THE ANATOMY OF A DECEPTION

*A Reconstruction and Analysis
of the Decision to Invade Iraq*

Robert A. Abele

University Press of America,® Inc.
Lanham · Boulder · New York · Toronto · Plymouth, UK

Copyright © 2010 by
University Press of America,® Inc.
4501 Forbes Boulevard
Suite 200
Lanham, Maryland 20706
UPA Acquisitions Department (301) 459-3366

Estover Road
Plymouth PL6 7PY
United Kingdom

All rights reserved
Printed in the United States of America
British Library Cataloging in Publication Information Available

Library of Congress Control Number: 2009928799
ISBN: 978-0-7618-4740-3 (paperback : alk. paper)
eISBN: 978-0-7618-4741-0

∞™ The paper used in this publication meets the minimum
requirements of American National Standard for Information
Sciences—Permanence of Paper for Printed Library Materials,
ANSI Z39.48-1992

Contents

Preface	v
Chapter One: Iraq and Contemporary *Realpolitik*	1
Chapter Two: The Arguments of the Progenitors of the Invasion of Iraq	13
Chapter Three: Refutation of the Arguments Supporting the Invasion	27
Chapter Four: The Ethical Case against the Conduct of the Invasion and Occupation of Iraq	51
Chapter Five: International Law and the Invasion of Iraq	77
Chapter Six: Preparing for the Next Deception	91
Bibliography	119
Index	125
About the Author	127

Preface

This book is a reconstruction of the public dialogue that ended with the United States collectively making the decision to invade and occupy the sovereign nation of Iraq. However, contrary to the implications of the title, this book essentially looks forward, not backward. Or rather, it looks backward *in order to* look forward, by asking what we can do to avoid falling prey to presidential and media manipulation in order to gain support for attacking a country that has done us no wrong? In other words, this book is about thinking critically about going to war by examining critically what the public debate was concerning the invasion and occupation of Iraq.

While much has since been discovered and written about the ostensive reasons for the invasion, most prominently weapons of mass destruction and the need to establish democracy, this book attempts to use only documents and articles involved in the public decision making process prior to March 19, 2003, the day the U.S. moved into Iraq. Where sources beyond this date are used, they were deliberately chosen only when they did not affect the overall argument. The point of limiting resources to the debate prior to this date is twofold. First, by demonstrating the parameters and content of the debate at the time, one may see the structure of the decision-making process that was done by those who lobbied for war, and those who were opposed to it. This will have the consequence of opening up the structure of the public debate on the invasion, and allow us to examine how it was we were led war by our nation's leaders. It will be argued here that the structure of the public case made for invading Iraq showed itself *at that time* to be a manipulation of evidence for a predetermined conclusion. This is not an earth-shattering thesis by those who are studied in this issue, but nearly two-thirds of American citizens were not convinced of this at the time of the war. Even now, there are still many who are not persuaded by this thesis. But by recognizing the manipulation of evidence *as it occurred*, by reconstructing it, we may perhaps be in a position to challenge national leadership more strongly and in more united fashion by recognizing the patterns of deception which lead to war. It is assumed here that deception does not have to be engaged in by the use of deliberate lies, but can be a one-sided selection of evidence intended to support a given conclusion, while ignoring or dismissing counter evidence.

The second point of recapturing the debate at the time and not in retrospect is to provide an ethical analysis of the decision-making structure and content used to go to war. It is hoped that by unabashedly taking the position that the decision-making was not done openly and honestly by our leaders, it will make a contribution both to post-invasion debate and also, hopefully, allow us to prevent being led down the path to war again without forcing leaders to make their case and to come clean with their *raison de guerre*. It is among the gravest of decisions a country can make to declare war on another country, and the debate leading in that direction must be done carefully, with the burden of proof of the need for war resting squarely on the shoulders of those who want to move the country in that direction. Even then, with international legal sanctions against one country invading another country which does not present an imminent threat, there must be a presumption against war that must be defeated by those who are rabid for a fight. That is the thesis of the analysis performed in this book, and it will be seen that these rational and ethical parameters to warmaking were not followed in the decision of the United States government to go to war against Iraq. Nor, incidentally, have these strictures been followed since.

The reason for the turn in American support for the war from 70% to 30% in favor has not been a new ethical consciousness or even a sense that we were manipulated in the decision-making process. Rather, the war didn't work: it didn't achieve the ends virtually guaranteed by our leaders during the decision-making process, of an easy victory and a welcome approbation as liberators. It is hoped that by retrospectively examining the debate, it will reignite a spark of an ethical consciousness that will be the normative presupposition for future debates, as well as giving rebirth to the rational requirement of a preponderance of the evidence before one offers ones support to such a monumental decision and undertaking.

In order to accomplish this task, we must begin with a synopsis of what philosophers have called "The Just War Theory" as a base for reinvigorating moral discussion concerning war and the decision to engage in it.

Is it possible for ethical principles to play a crucial role in the decision of a country to go to war? Can ethics place realistic constraints on the conduct of wars? In attempting to answer these questions, this essay applies what has come to be called the "Just War Theory" to the decision to invade Iraq in March of 2003. Perhaps the term "theory" is a misnomer, for the ethical limits in the tradition of the justified war are more a method than a theory in the technical sense. Rather, "Just War Theory" refers to a series of ethical limitations to warfare that have been developed in the course of Western history which have been held to be the moral norm for determining whether or not a given war is (or was) ethically permissible. Thus, perhaps it would be better to refer to this history as the Just War Tradition. One way or another, these criteria have developed along two levels. The first level is concerned with both the beginning and the ends of war; that is, with what constitutes morally legitimate reasons for engaging in war. This is referred to as the *jus ad bellum*. The second level is *jus in bello*, and is concerned with the *means* of war: whether certain actions are proportional to the ends, and whether or not the innocent in war are sufficiently protected from attack.

In general, the way that the Just War Theory addresses the issue of war is to begin with the admission of the partial truths of two mutually contradictory doctrines, each of which rejects the possibility that ethics can be brought to bear on war. The first of these arguments is known as "Realism" or *Realpolitik*. This philosophy maintains that ethics cannot be applied to politics at all, thus *a fortiori* not to warfare. After all, as General William Tecumseh Sherman described it, "War is hell." The second philosophical position on war is the polar opposite of Realism. It is usually called "Pacifism," which, like Realism, maintains that ethics and warfare have no relation to one another. Unlike Realism, however, Pacifism makes its claims on the grounds that the value of human life is absolute, such that no killing of persons--especially not the killing that war entails--can ever be ethical. This type of argument maintains a moral absolutism concerning human life. Applied to politics, the absolutist position fails to account for the problem of morally ambiguous situations, in which moral goods conflict and no clear moral course of action presents itself. The Just War Theory is itself nothing less than a negative rejoinder to absolutist ethics of the pacifistic kind: the end *can* sometimes justify the means if the moral value(s) which constitute the ends of war are sufficient for their moral priority over the values which would be appealed to in order to condemn the act of war *in toto*.

The specific points of examination of warfare by ethical principles concern the *jus ad bellum*, literally, the "laws to war." This general grouping of ethical parameters for deciding to engage in war include the criteria of just cause, right intention, proper authority, last resort, probability of success, and the proportionality of the overall war. The *jus in bello* criteria, literally "laws in war," include the proportionality of specific actions and also protection of noncombatants from direct and intentional attacks.

The *jus ad bellum* criteria may be summarily defined as follows.

Just cause—This is the main criterion of the Just War Tradition, and it deals with the requirements to be met before a state engages in war. These requirements are usually said to be self-defense against a real attack, and defense against an imminent attack. This not only presupposes the moral legitimacy of the state, but there is much discussion today concerning whether humanitarian intervention or pre-emptive strikes are just causes. We will not delve too deeply into these specific issues here. Our main focus will be on Iraq.

Right Intention—One can easily see that the just cause condition heavily influences, if it does not determine, right intention. The right intention requires that war be fought only to correct a current injustice or an engaged or forthcoming military attack. Acts of military aggression are ruled out by this criterion, as well as by that of just cause.

Proper Authority—Only state authority can launch a war. How this state authority works to do so varies between countries, but the point of this requirement is that only those state authorities who are so constituted by a state constitution are entitled to decide to go to war, not individuals or other corporate entities.

Last resort—This condition requires that all peaceful alternatives to war be reasonably exhausted before the war is commenced. While some criticize this criterion on the grounds that it could never be fulfilled, the operative term "reasonable" presents the proper meaning of this constraint on war.

Probability of success—A state should not go to war unless there is strong evidence that they can win the war they are contemplating. This can be interpreted more along pragmatic than ethical lines, but taking a nation into a war doomed to failure would cost many lives increase suffering and even threaten the nation's existence unnecessarily. These concerns are distinctly moral.

Proportionality—This requires that the overall good from the war outweigh the evil that the war will cause. This is necessarily predictive and consequential in form, but it expresses a crucial limitation on war's conduct.

The *jus in bello* criteria, meaning "laws in war," is directed at the specific actions in war. Thus, it concerns the conduct of soldiers and their commanders.

Proportionality—Any given military action must be constrained by the goal it attempts to achieve. This means that the use of weapons of mass destruction, for instance, nuclear or biological weapons, not be used because they go beyond the legitimate ends of a battle by allowing the destruction exceed what is needed for victory.

Discrimination/Noncombatant Immunity—This element requires that soldiers make sure they target only those who seek to harm them in some way. This means that civilians are immune to direct attack. There are many questions and gray areas that are involved here, but it nonetheless remains a widely-held ethical criterion.

For a war to be considered a "just war," each of these criteria must be met. This is the ethical scheme by which we will examine the invasion of Iraq. In addition, we will be bringing to bear on the public discussion for war with Iraq the requirements of rationality which, together with the ethical limitations on warfare, present a powerful set of tools for analyzing the arguments both for and against a proposed and then conducted war. We will see that, by the application of these two general categories of thinking, the content of the debate concerning the Iraq war was both unethical and irrational, as has been the conduct of the war once we engaged in it. The case will be clearly made that, with gross violations of these criteria as well as international law, the "pro war" argument was shallow and insufficient to send our country to war. That is one of the reasons we are still bogged down there, six years into the invasion: lack of thought about it, and lack of concern with ethics and law. President Bush once referred to those we are fighting as "lawless." One of the most important lessons of this book will hopefully be that we cannot war on those who are "lawless" when we ourselves are lawless. This book is intended to challenge us to learn to debate such important issues more deeply, more reflectively, and with more ethical commitment than we did prior to the U.S. invasion of Iraq. If we do not commit ourselves to that, and set about righting the wrongs done in the public debate regarding Iraq, we will find ourselves in many more wars to come, for no other reason than the self-interests of those who bring us the wars to enhance their own profit and/or power. That this is a direct threat to democracy should come as no surprise; that it is a direct threat to continued republicanism in America itself, especially due to its economic draining of the country's treasury, is a real threat to which Americans must wake up. This book intends to assist in that rousing of people from their intellectual and ethical slumber.

Chapter One
Iraq and Contemporary *Realpolitik*

Introduction to the Iraq Issue

The invasion of Iraq must be seen in the context of a much wider view of the Middle East and of world politics. For thirty years, the United States has been drawing a military noose around the Mideast. This practice made its way into the public dialogue in 1975, in an article in *Harper's* magazine entitled "Seizing Arab Oil." The thesis of the article was that the U.S. would maintain its current lifestyle and prosper simply by overtaking the Mideast oil fields. According to journalist Robert Dreyfus, this thirty year-old goal was accomplished in five steps.[1] First the "Rapid Deployment Force" was created. This was a Carter administration creation of a military unit of several thousand that could be rapidly sent to the Middle East to protect American oil interests.

Second, in the Reagan administration, the Rapid Deployment force became the "Central Command." This shift of vision moved from rapid deployment to permanent military bases in and around the Persian Gulf. To achieve this aim, Reagan sold billions of dollars worth of arms to Saudi Arabia. The navy also developed a "Joint Task Force-Middle East" to escort oil tankers through the Gulf.

Step three, according to Dreyfus, was the 1991 Gulf War. Prior to the invasion of Kuwait by Saddam Hussein, the U.S. had been unable to persuade the Saudis to allow U.S. military bases in their country. After the invasion, the U.S. not only got its bases, but also profited from the sales of $43 billion worth of weapons to the Saudis. The result of U.S. victory in the Gulf war, and the need to enforce the no-fly zone in northern Iraq, allowed the U.S. to engage in a massive military build-up in the Gulf. The use of military bases in Turkey and Saudi Arabia were used to accomplish its aims in northern Iraq.

Step four commenced with the invasion of Afghanistan, and step five was the invasion of Iraq, both done to secure American control of the region.

According to the book by journalist Bob Woodward, *Plan of Attack*, just five days after the event of 9/11/01, President Bush clearly indicated to National Security Advisor Condoleeza Rice that he wanted a pretext to remove Saddam Hussein from power. This story has been corroborated by Richard Clarke, former Clinton and Bush National Security Advisor, who tells the same story in his book, *Against All Enemies*. Woodward goes on to relate how President Bush, on November 21, 2001, just 72 days after the events of 9/11, cornered Donald Rumsfeld, then Secretary of Defense, and pressured him regarding his plans for attacking Iraq. From there the physical construction began to make the attack possible in Kuwait (e.g. runways and pipelines). Even though, as Woodward relates, Mr. Bush knew that the evidence that Saddam Hussein had weapons of mass destruction was flimsy at best, by early January of 2003, the President made the decision to engage the U.S. war machine against Iraq, without obtaining the advise of key members of his cabinet.

Now that the U.S. controls the oil supply of both Iraq and Afghanistan, the Bush administration is in the process of doing what the neoconservative think tanks have advocated they do: divide the oil reserves of country among private American oil companies.

The economic and geo-political interests that propelled the Mideast takeover by the U.S. military reveal clearly the philosophy that underpins it. The term "Realpolitik" is a French word that American pragmatists simply refer to as "Realism." This term advocates a political philosophy which maintains that politics does not involve the use of universal moral principles, but rather revolves around "the concept of interest defined in terms of power."[2] It is this presupposition that infuses the "Realists" with their policy formulations and understandings. When it comes to the invasion and occupation of Iraq by the United States, understanding the philosophy of Realism is important to understanding the real reasons for the invasion. We will see those reasons unfold as we examine the views of the architects of the invasion. That philosophy is embodied in a group that is called by contemporary colloquial term "neocon" (as in "neoconservative"). A more accurate term for this group of men (no women are involved in this project) who have for years advocated American hegemony in the world is neo-Straussian, since by their own admission they owe the philosophical ideas that support such economic and military opportunism, as shown in the invasions of Afghanistan and Iraq, to the philosopher Leo Strauss.

Neocon Influence on U.S. Foreign Policy: Leo Strauss and His Followers

It is difficult to understand fully the Bush administration foreign policy without knowing something about the group of his advisors now euphemistically referred to as "the neocons." This group, along with their intellectual colleagues in academia, are admitted followers of the philosopher Leo Strauss (1899—1973) of the University of Chicago. The neocons include Allan Bloom, Clarence Thomas, Robert Bork, William Bennett, Francis Fukuyama, Paul Wolfowitz, Elliott Abrams, Alan Keyes, and William Kristol—all well-known names in politics today. Since they claim Strauss for their intellectual heritage, it is important to examine the political philosophy Strauss taught.

Straussian political philosophy is based on the thesis that western culture is in crisis, in that the State no longer inculcates virtue in its citizens. Thus, visionary moral leaders are needed. In this sense, Strauss was a strong intellectual elitist: the philosopher (the moral state leader) was above the city (citizens), and not connected to the city, similar to the "philosopher king" of Plato in the latter's *Republic*. The philosopher is the virtuous leader because s/he understands "the eternal causes of the whole."[3] Thus, there is a difference between the prephilosophical understanding of citizens and the philosopher's need for detachment from the city.

Yet, the philosopher lies to the city (by using "noble lies") about the close relationship of leader virtue and city values, all the while understanding the groundlessness of the city's virtues (i.e. that city's virtues are necessarily conditional).

The central category for Straussian political analysis was the "regime," defined by Strauss as "the order or form of society."[4] Thus, the regime is a specific way of life, of living together. Although Strauss resurrected the term "regime" from Greek political thought, it will become easily discernible that "regime" meant something different to his neocon students.

Strauss's main concern in his text, *What is Political Philosophy?*, is to trace (and reject) the movement of western political thinking from virtue to freedom (i.e. from classical to modern political thinking). In other words, he finds reason to repudiate the shift in Western political philosophy from the Athenian concept of proper political actions—that knowledge of the good/virtue is prior to the right—to the emphasis on individual freedom and plurality of goods. It is this shift to freedom which resulted in the loss of the classical conception of the virtuous leader who knows virtue above his or her freedom to do good or evil.

The Classical Solution

Strauss accuses Western political philosophy of breeding positivism, historicism, and relativism. As he frames the problem,

> historicism rejects the question of the good society, that is to say, of the good society, because of the essentially historical character of society and of human thought. . . . The crucial issue concerns the status of those permanent characteristics of humanist, such as the distinction between the noble and the base. . . . It was the contempt for these permanencies which permitted the most radical historicist in 1933 to submit to, or rather to welcome . . . the verdict of the least wise and least moderate part of his nation.[5]

Thus, for Strauss, Western liberal democracy has bred fascism, particularly in the form of Hitler's Nazi Germany.

Strauss argues that the classics (i.e. Plato and Aristotle) provide a solution to the problem produced by liberal democracy in giving birth to relativism, nihilism and fascism. It comes in the admonition to return to "nature" and to "the permanent thing" such as virtue and knowledge of the good. For the Greeks, politics was natural, not human-created: "A human being is said to be natural if he is guided by nature rather than convention or inherited opinion."[6]

In addition, Athenian political philosophy was nontraditional, since no tradition had developed yet. Therefore, it was "new" and fresh as never before. The political philosophy of the Greeks "look[s] further afield in the same direction as the enlightened citizens or statesmen."[7] Because they use the same language as statesmen and citizens, classical political philosophy is comprehensive in that it is both political theory and political skill. That is, it is open to as well as transcends the legal and institutional dynamics of life in the *polis*.

Modern political philosophy, on the other hand, has a derivative character, which Strauss defines as a distance from the primary issues. The result is that for modern political philosophy, abstractness is the starting point, and concreteness is the end for which it aims.[8] But the concrete at which it arrives is still an abstraction, an intellectual reconstruction of reality and thus still an idea, not a lived world. The example Strauss adduces is the "I-Thou" relation of Martin Buber, which Strauss believes was predicated on the Cartesian "cogito." This stands in stark contrast to the equivalent Greek conception of human relations in the *polis* as being that of "friends."

For Strauss, Plato's *Laws* is the best example of classical political philosophy. Human legislators depend on the whole social and political order, the *politeia*, the regime. The cause of the laws is the regime. Thus, the guiding theme of political philosophy is the regime rather than the laws. The definition of regime is the order/form of the life of a society. Thus, a "regime" is a specific way of living together; its moral taste.

"*Politeia*" is the expression of "regime." Life is activity directed toward some goal; social life is an activity which is directed toward such a goal as can only be pursued by society. In order to pursue it, society must be organized in a manner consistent with the goal, and the authoritative human beings must be akin to that goal. The political leader must know the good to which the regime naturally moves.

For Strauss, the fatherland or nation is the matter; the regime is the form, and form is higher in dignity than matter. Thus, the best regime is higher in dignity than the nation. Pursuit of the best regime, then, should be the goal of political philosophy in the classical mode.

The problem, as Strauss recognizes, is that classical political philosophy is anti-democratic and thus judged to be inferior or even bad by the political standards of today. To this rejoinder, Strauss reminds us that Plato's *Republic* does hold democracy to be *equal to* the best regime, and that the rejection of democracy by the classics is based on stable and predominant old families and the proper aim of the political life: virtue, not freedom. The reason is that

> Freedom as a goal is ambiguous, because it is freedom for evil as well as for good. Virtue emerges normally only through education...and this requires leisure . . . but leisure in its turn requires some degree of wealth.

Thus, "democracy, or rule of the majority, is government by the uneducated."[9]

The superiority of the Greeks, argues Strauss, is that they realized that humans need education in virtue to adhere to it, as opposed to Rousseau, who believed that all moral knowledge is supplied by the conscience. Since it has been "agreed in history" that democracy must be rule by the educated, universal education becomes the requirement for its success. However, this presupposes that an economy of plenty exists; and the economy of plenty presupposes that technology has been liberated from moral and political control. This is the main difference between the classical and modern approaches to democracy: it "consists exclusively in a different estimate of the virtues of technology. [The classical] prophecy that the emancipation of technology, of the arts, from moral and political control would lead to disaster or to the dehumanization of man has not yet been refuted."[10] The Greeks had it right, according to Strauss: only a minority of wealthy people had the leisure to cultivate character, learn virtue, and thus lead the regime toward its natural goal.

One can see the need in Strauss's thinking for a strong and centralized government to keep the arts under close scrutiny and control. That is one of the reasons the strong leader must know the good, must know virtue. But democracy has failed humanity in that regard, according to Strauss, for at least two reasons. First, what is called education today is not "education proper—"i.e. the formation of character. Rather, education is now "instruction and training." Second, any education that is done as character formation—i.e. "the good man"—today is about being a "good sport" or being cooperative with others, and is thus insufficient for the good of the regime.

That is why Strauss maintains that modernity has failed and bred nihilism in its wake. Whereas in the classical conception, "the goal of political life is virtue, and the order most conducive to virtue is the aristocratic republic," the modern emphasis has become that of freedom and plurality, in which "we find a great variety of fundamentally different philosophies . . . hav[ing] a fundamental principle in common . . . rejection of the classical scheme as unrealistic."[11] As he traces the movement toward nihilism that results from emphasizing freedom over virtue, he discovers its origin in the "three waves of modernity:" Machiavelli, Hobbes, and Locke; Rousseau and the German Idealists; and Nietzsche. Each of these, in his turn, effected a break with the classical tradition:

- Machiavelli with his critique of religion and classical morality;
- Hobbes with his conception of the depravity of human nature, which is very un-Greek-like;
- Locke with his mitigation of Hobbes by beginning with self-preservation in the face of evil humanity;
- Rousseau, who limits license horizontally by the license of others instead of vertically by knowledge of the good; and

- Nietzsche, who denied that rational legitimation was possible and who thus argued for "the solitary creator who gives a new law unto himself," and thus had no conception of political responsibility.

Finally, for Strauss,

> Modern thought reaches it culmination, its highest self-consciousness, in the most radical historicism, i.e., in explicitly condemning to oblivion the notion of eternity . . . or, in other words, estrangement from man's deepest desire and therewith from the primary issues.[12]

It is this contempt for modernism that the neocons learned from Strauss. The modernist/liberal rejection of the directedness of human nature to the permanent good, the rejection of republican aristocracy, in which the leaders know the good, the emphasis on pluralism of goods instead of a single permanent good, were all foci of the Straussian negation of modernism that would be put to work in both the minds and actions of his disciples.

Analysis of Strauss

The purpose in presenting the philosophy of Strauss is to demonstrate the link between Strauss's brand of conservative thinking and that of the neocons, who were the ones who proposed and defended the invasion and occupation of Iraq. However, a few comments about Straussian thinking are in order before we move to his neocon disciples.

The first problem in Straussian political philosophy comes with the term "natural" as it is applied to human nature. That humans have a single nature is part of the modern critique of classical thinking, and Strauss simply does not address this issue. But calling something "natural," particularly as applied to human nature, raises the inevitable question as to whose definition of human nature is the properly "natural" one. As is well known, Aristotle's understanding of what is "natural" to humans supported slavery.[13] Nietzsche understands the concept of the "I" variously as a product of language, and/or as an ethical need to be responsible for our actions.[14] Thus, any reference to human "nature" will be a linguistic an ethical one, based on what Nietzsche (and his postmodern followers) calls a "prejudice," not a metaphysical given.

Most importantly, Strauss accuses the modern philosophers of stripping the notion of "transcendence" or "eternity" from their understanding of the good in society. In its place, Strauss says, modern political philosophy has as its main premise "to become the master and owner of nature."[15] But surely this is an incomplete characterization of the moderns. Locke, for instance, in his *Two Treatises of Government*, states that the natural law does not originate in the free will of individuals, but is rational and by nature a part of us.[16] This likewise holds true for his essay *Essays on the Law of Nature*, where he states that natural law is "the decree of the divine will discernible by the light of nature and indicating what is and what is not in conformity with rational nature."[17] Thus, it has an objective characteristic, much the same in form although different in content from classical theory.

Furthermore, continuing from this last point, his reading of the modern philosophers is incomplete. For example, Locke does not simply "take over the fundamental scheme of Hobbes and change it only in one point...acquisitiveness."[18] Locke argued for a scheme of equality and representative government that was more complex than, and well beyond, that of Hobbes. Locke held that since all people are by nature human, and equally human, they ought to be treated equally.[19] Moreover, Hobbes's theory of natural law terminated in the right of absolute rule of the Leviathan, while Locke's theory condemned it by replacing it with the notion of the social contract in which political power begins with and always redounds to the people. Thus, monarchy, especially an authoritarian monarchy such as advocated by Hobbes, is anathema to Locke because it is unnatural.[20]

Third, Strauss leans fairly heavily on the notion of "permanence" as it applies to the good or virtue. Philosophy is certainly the pursuit of the good, but that does not mean that it ever achieves its destination. The longing for eternal virtue is certainly one which Strauss and his opponents can share; that the moderns have cut that longing out completely we have already seen to be false. Strauss is right that it becomes increasingly secularized, but that does not mean it has been eclipsed.

Moreover, Strauss's use of an exclusive disjunction between the ancients and moderns is too strong: they do not have to be interpreted as being polarities. For example, the natural law tradition of the classical theory is brought over into the natural rights theory of the moderns. Since, as we have seen, Locke does not place the origin of natural law in the free will, there is no need to conclude with Strauss that classical and modern political philosophy have diverged completely from one another.

Finally, for Strauss, Western liberal democracy has bred fascism, particularly in the form of Hitler's Nazi Germany. Strauss would have difficulty in creating a more detailed argument for this accusation, because Hitler had nothing but contempt for parliamentary democracy, the masses, and the truth, advocating as he did lies and myths to placate the masses. It would seem far closer to the truth to say that the neocon vision of politics that is born from Strauss's thinking was itself akin to fascism. For example, neocon Irving Kristol, in an article entitled "The New Populism: Not to Worry,"[21] suggests that the neocon movement use democracy to defeat liberty and liberalism—i.e. make the charge that "liberty is licentiousness;" that liberalism undermines religion and leads to crime, drugs, homosexuality, children out of wedlock, etc. To this it might be added, says Kristol, that liberalism is soft on communism [and now terrorism]. The neoconservative response to these problems allegedly bred by liberalism is for a Straussian-type of elitism.

Enter the Neocons

That Strauss had a significant impact on his nascent neocon students is not an understatement may be seen clearly in the themes they brought forward from their master, with their own twist added. Foremost among them is the use of the "noble lie" in U.S. military adventurism. Their exaggerations of the power of al Qaeda and also the need to invade Iraq because of its growing military power stand as a shining example of their version of the "noble lie." They also brought Straussian elitism with them in the form of economic class divisions. Their Straussian project, called "The Project for a New American Century," elaborated their philosophy (PNAC).[22] This organization was founded as a neo-conservative "think tank" by William Kristol in 1997, with the stated goal of promoting American global hegemony. Its members at the time included Paul Wolfowitz, William Bennett, Dick Cheney, Richard Perle, Donald Rumsfeld, Richard Armitage, John Bolton, and Lewis "Scooter" Libby.

As secretive as they have been accused of being, they nonetheless produced key documents outlining their philosophy. Chronologically, the first significant document they presented of their philosophy is entitled "Defense Planning Guidance." Written in 1992 by Paul Wolfowitz and embraced by Dick Cheney, this document called for U.S. foreign policy "to prevent the re-emergence of a new rival" in world power. It also advocated the use of preemptive military action on the part of the United States. Most studied opinions refer to this principle as "preventive" action, since preemptive action requires a direct threat from another country, while this neocon doctrine urges prevention of the very possibility of such a threat. It calls on the U.S. to maintain a massive nuclear weapons system, and that it be ready to act unilaterally, working with other countries only so long as a crisis lasts in which they need those other countries.

In 1997, they released their "Statement of Principles," in which they called for significant increases in U.S. military spending, coupled with a foreign policy of challenging regimes hostile to U.S. interests, and promoting and then preserving an international order friendly to U.S. interests.

In 1998, they wrote a letter to then-President Clinton expressing their displeasure with his foreign policy and advocating that he take on their own views. According to the letter, the main U.S. foreign policy goal should be the elimination of Saddam Hussein. Their subargument: because in the future it may become impossible to know whether or not he has "weapons of mass destruction" (WMD's), the future may hold a threat to U.S. oil interests. Therefore, the letter concluded, Saddam *is* a threat of great magnitude. Therefore, the U.S. should ignore the U.N. and eliminate him.

One of their most significant documents was released in 2000. Entitled "Rebuilding America's Defenses," it called for America to seek to extend its power and leadership in the world by maintaining the preeminence of U.S. military forces. In addition, it advocated the redeployment of U.S. forces at new and permanent bases in Southeast Europe and Southeast Asia. Iraq, Iran, Syria, and North Korea are clearly named as primary short-term targets for U.S. military intervention. The document advocated that the U.S. abandon working with the U.N., by using the phrase "constabulary duties" which "demand American political leadership rather than that of the United Nations."

Furthermore, the U.S. military should be enlarged and become "globalized," ready to maintain U.S. national security in critical regions of the world. It called on the U.S. to abandon ABM treaty between the U.S. and Russia (which the U.S. did in 2002); to strive to control outer space by the creation of a new military service, the "U.S. Space Forces," and to engage in ". . . advanced forms of biological warfare that can target specific genotypes may transform biological warfare from the realm of terror to a politically useful tool." This will allow the U.S. military to target one race over another for attack (e.g. Iranians vs. Saudi Arabs).

But the most chilling part of this document advocated a quick process to engage these goals:

> Further, the process of transformation, even if it brings revolutionary change, is likely to be a long one, absent some catastrophic and catalyzing event—like a new Pearl Harbor.

These ideas finally worked their way into official U.S. policy in *The National Security Strategy of the United States* (2002).

Analysis of Straussian Neocon Philosophy

To even the most casual reader of these documents, the philosophy advocated is clearly that of imperialism in the highest degree. The term "imperialism" is usually defined along the lines of the extension of the power and legal dominion of one state over another, and this is precisely what the documents from the PNAC openly advocate.[23] Second, they rely almost entirely on military power to achieve their goals. No economic cooperation, no treaties, no diplomacy; just raw power. This might work on playgrounds with bullies, but in world politics it is incredibly short-sighted because it creates more animosities and struggles against it than does diplomacy, and it risks more violence and terrorism by its use of military might to get its way in the world. But international politics today requires cooperation and cooperation requires mutual interests.

Third, the drain on the U.S. economy for such actions will be immense. For example, in 2000, the U.S. spent $281 billion on the military, more than the next eleven nations combined.[24] Further, it has been widely estimated that the Iraq war will cost upwards of $1.2 trillion.

Finally, according to Austin Bramwell, a former neocon, the neocon philosophy betrays a superficial Foreign Policy. What conditions cause threats to emerge to the U.S.? They are never defined in neocon philosophy or writings. What threats emerge from the Middle East and how do the alleged conditions cause them? How do you change the alleged conditions that cause the threat?

Finally, the connection between Iraq and 9/11 and Iraq and terrorism are left undefined.[25]

If the neocon philosophy is fraught with superficialities and incompleteness, that did not stop it from rising to the ranks of the preferred philosophy of the most powerful government in the world: the United States, through the auspices of its current Vice President, Dick Cheney, and former Deputy Defense Director PaulWolfowitz.

Notes

1. Dreyfus, Robert, "The Thirty-year Itch," *Mother Jones*, March/April, 2001, pgs. 41—45.

2. From Hans Morgenthau, one of the early 20th-century American Realists;.see his *Politics Among Nations* (New York: Alfred Knopf, 1954), p. 5. Realism is as old as political institutions themselves. See, for example, Thucydides, *History of the Peloponnesian Wars*. Plato also dealt with Realism in his dialogue *Gorgias*, through the character of Callicles.

3. Unless otherwise noted, this examination of Strauss is developed from his text What is Political Philosophy? (Chicago: University of Chicago Press, 1959). Hereafter abbreviated as *WPP*.

4. WPP, p. 34.
5. Ibid. p. 27.
6. Ibid., p. 27.
7. Ibid.

8. Although not a contemporary of Strauss, a good example of what Strauss means by the abstractness of modern political theory may be seen in the political philosophy of John Rawls. In his book *A Theory of Justice*, Rawls argues from abstract the premises of an initial situation in which persons do not know their social status or conditions. From this "Original Position," Rawls concludes two abstract principles of justice to guide deliberations once the concrete is reestablished.

9. WPP, p. 37.
10. Ibid., p. 37.
11. Ibid., p. 40.
12. Ibid., p. 55.
13. Aristotle, *Politics*, V & VI.

14. For language and the sense of ego, see *Twilight of the Idols*, 5; for the ethical sense that generates an "I," see *Genealogy of Morals*. Postmodernists such as Michel Foucault follow this line of Nietzschean analysis; something Strauss seems to fear would happen.

15. WPP, p. 55.
16. *Two Treatises of Government*, 2.11, 2.4, 7, 22, 134—5, 149, 171.
17. *Essays on the Law of Nature*, p. 111.
18. WPP, p. 49.
19. John Locke, *Second Treatise of Government*, Ch. II, 4—6.

20. For Hobbes' notion of monarchy, see his *Leviathan*, Ch. 19. For Locke's rejection of such monarchy, see his *Second Treatise of Government*, n. 90. Incidentally, Locke does not advocate unlimited acquisition, as Strauss charges. Quite the contrary, property accumulation was to be limited to what a person could use, and was not to be wasted (II, 36).

21. *Wall Street Journal*, July 25, 1985.

22. Although now disbanded, their official web site is still available at www.pnac.org.

23. See, for example, Chalmers Johnson, in *Blowback* (New York: Metropolitan Books, 2000), p. 19.

24. Bookman, Jay, "The President's Real Goal in Iraq," *Information Clearinghouse*, September 29, 2002.

25. Austin Bramwell, "Good-bye to All That," The American Conservative, November 20, 2006.

Chapter Two
The Arguments of the Progenitors of the Invasion of Iraq

The Official U.S. Government Case for Going to War with Iraq

In a speech at the United Nations on September 12, 2002, President Bush made his first public pitch for going to war with Iraq, followed by a similar speech in Cincinnati, Ohio in October. The details of his accusations against Iraq in both speeches were sketchy and uncorroborated by evidence. Instead, he went right to the appeal to fear that the administration would use to conjure up enough terror in the American people to support the invasion: Iraq was "reconstituting its nuclear weapons program." From this point on, layers upon layers of accusations would be made by the Bush administration against Iraq. What follows is not a chronological summary of the charges, but a content summary. Here the case the Bush people made for the necessity of invading Iraq:[1]

1. Iraq "did not file a complete and accurate declaration of his weapons to the U.N. and has not cooperated fully with U.N. inspections."
2. Iraq "has not complied with Resolution 1441,
3. Iraq has "mobile units producing biological weapons," including a U.N. estimate of 26,000 liters of anthrax and another U.N. estimate of perhaps more than double the 19,000 liters of botulinum toxin that they declared.
4. Iraq continues to produce chemical weapons, such as VX nerve gas, for which "the U.N. concluded" that 1.5 tons was unaccounted.
5. "UNMOVIC has reported that Iraq failed to provide evidence to account for 1,000 tons of mustard gas, 550 mustard gasfilled munitions, and hundreds of biological weapons-capable aerial bombs."
6. "Iraq has repeatedly sought to illegally procure aluminum tubes . . . that are consistent with its pre-Gulf War design to enrich uranium."
7. Iraq had engaged in multiple test flights of the al-Samoud 2, a ballistic missile system that exceeds the 150 kilometer limit set by the U.N.

The CIA, for its part, produced an intelligence document entitled "Iraq's Weapons of Mass Destruction Programs" in October, 2002. In that study, they not only reiterated the charges made by the State Department, above, but added a few of their own. Here are the additional charges made in that document:

1. "All key aspects—R&D, production, and weaponization—of Iraq's offensive BW [biological weapons] program are active and most elements are larger and more advanced than they were before the Gulf war."

2. Iraq has "orchestrated an extensive concealment and deception campaign to hide incriminating documents and material that precluded resolution of key issues pertaining to its WMD [weapons of mass destruction] program."

It is interesting to note that in nearly every judgment and analysis made in this document, the CIA authors were very careful in their use of nuance, using such hedging terms as "probably," "suggest," "may," "most," etc.

In addition to these "official" charges, various high-ranking members of the Bush Cabinet busily made similar charges in public speeches and articles. For example, Condolezza Rice penned an op-ed piece in the *New York Times* explaining why it was necessary to go to war with Iraq. In that piece, Rice stated that Iraq had failed to disarm; that its 12,200 page report was a "lie;" that Iraq attempted to get uranium from abroad; that it had "thousands of gallons of anthrax and other biological weapons," and other standard administration claims.

But the *coup de grace* for the Bush case for invading Iraq came when Colin Powell, then Secretary of State, on February 6, 2003, made a major presentation to the United Nations Security Council allegedly detailing the evidence the U.S. had that Iraq was not complying with U.N. resolutions 687 and 1441. His appearance at the U.N. was intended to sway the Security Council to give the U.S. permission to attack Iraq. Here is a synopsis of the main points Powell made in that speech. For sake of organization, I have divided his presentation into what appear to be his main theses.

His first thesis is that Iraq is not complying with U.N. Resolution 1441. This Resolution, written by the United States and Britain, passed on November 8, 2002. It gave Iraq "a final opportunity" to comply with Resolution 687 in particular. The latter resolution, passed in 1991, after the U.S. forced Iraqi troops to withdraw from Kuwait, called for Iraq to cease production of weapons of mass destruction and make reparations to Kuwait. But 1441 was the Resolution which the U.S. used to request the imprimatur of the international community to invade Iraq in 2003. The evidence Powell presented that Iraq was not complying with former U.N. resolutions included the following arguments:

1. General Powell played an audiotape which he stated was recorded on November 26, 2002. There was no corroborating evidence of the date or parties recorded, but in the tape, the two parties apparently discuss how to modify a vehicle before Mohamed El Baradei, U.N. inspector, arrives. The tape contains rather vague references, but it was nonetheless submitted as evidence.

2. A second tape was played, in which two unnamed parties discuss hiding "forbidden ammunition." Powell concludes from these two tapes that the Iraqi

officials are engaged in "a system of hiding things and moving things out of the way."

3. Powell asserted that Saddam Hussein has "a higher committee for monitoring the inspection team." Powell concludes from this that Iraq meant "not to cooperate" with the U.N. inspectors.

4. Iraq made a 12,200-page declaration of its weapons to the U.N. Security Council on December 7, 2002, which Dr. Hans Blix, chief U.N. inspector, declared to be "rich in volume but poor in information and practically devoid of new evidence." Powell concludes from this that the declaration was "false."

5. Powell continues with a very vague and unsubstantiated claim: "Orders were issued to Iraq's security organizations as well as to Saddam Hussein's own office to hide all correspondence with the Organization of Military Industrialization. That is the organization that oversees Iraq's weapons of mass destruction activities. Make sure there are no documents left which would connect you to the O.M.I."

6. Powell continues: "We know," he states, "that Saddam's son Qusay ordered the removal of all prohibited weapons from Saddam's numerous palace complexes," and "we know" that "scientists have hidden prohibited items in their homes."

7. Further: "Our sources tell us that in some cases the hard drives of computers at Iraqi weapons facilities were replaced." From this assertion, Powell concludes that they were hiding them from inspectors.

8. Next, Powell showed satellite photos which he claimed would be "hard for the average person to read," but which nevertheless showed missile launching equipment and locations, chemical bunkers, decontamination vehicles. Then Powell showed a photo which he said was of the same site, in which such things were now gone. Although no dates appeared on the photos, Powell assured the U.N. delegates that the second photo was taken on December 22, 2002, "as the U.N. inspection team is arriving."

9. Powell showed more photos which he maintained demonstrated Iraqi duplicity, but admitted that "we don't know precisely what Iraq was moving, but the inspectors already knew about these sites. So Iraq knew that they would be coming."

10. "Iraq also has refused to permit any U-2 recognizance flights that would give inspectors a better sense of what's being moved . . . a direct violation of operative Paragraph 7 of our Resolution 1441."

11. "Iraq has not complied with its obligation to allow immediate unimpeded, unrestricted and private access to all officials and other persons as required by Resolution 1441." Powell presents no evidence to support this contention.

Mr. Powell concludes from these bits of evidence that Iraq is engaged in "an active and systematic effort . . . to keep key materials and people from the inspectors, in direct violation of Resolution 1441." He reiterates that this is "a deliberate campaign.

Mr. Powell's second thesis is that Iraq has weapons of mass destruction. Here is his stated evidence:

1. Biological weapons must be there on the following grounds:
    a. It took UNSCOM four years to get Iraq to admit that it had them.
    b. In 1995, the quantities were vast.
    c. "Iraq declared 8,500 liters of anthrax, but UNSCOM estimates that Saddam Hussein could have produced 25,000 liters."
    d. In what Powell calls his "key point," he states that "the Iraqis have never accounted for all of the biological weapons they admitted they had and we know they had." He concludes that "this is all well documented," but presents no documentation.
    e. Powell charges Iraq with possessing "mobile production facilities used to make biological agents." His evidence for this assertion: "we have firsthand descriptions of biological weapons factories on wheels and on rails." From there, he appeals to unnamed "eyewitnesses." Powell added: "We know that Iraq has at least seven of these mobile biological agent factories . . . perhaps 18."
    f. Powell further charges that "Saddam Hussein has investigated dozens of biological agents, causing diseases such as gas gangrene, plague, typhus, tetanus, cholera, camel pox and hemorrhagic fever. And he has the wherewithal to develop smallpox." No evidence is presented to support these charges.

2. Iraq has chemical weapons. The evidence given by Powell to support this conclusion is as follows:
    a. "Saddam Hussein has used these horrific weapons on another country and on his own people."
    b. "Saddam Hussein has never accounted for vast amounts of chemical weaponry . . . [such as] 6,500 bombs from the Iran-Iraq war, UNMOVIC says the amount of chemical agent in them would be in the order of a thousand tons . . . We believe Saddam Hussein knows what he did with it and he has not come clean with the international community."
    c. "Iraq's record on chemical weapons is replete with lies."
    d. "We know that Iraq has embedded key portions of its illicit chemical weapons infrastructure within its legitimate civilian industry."
    e. Powell produced a satellite photo which he stated was taken in May, 2002, and used an unnamed "human source" who said that "movement of chemical weapons occurred at this site." He then produced a second photo, said to have been taken in July, 2002, which he said showed that the site had been bulldozed and the topsoil removed.
    f. "Our conservative estimate is that Iraq today has a stockpile of between 100 to 500 tons of chemical-weapons agent." Again, he presents no studies and no evidence to verify this estimate.
    g. "We have sources who tell us that [Hussein] recently has authorized his field commanders to use them [chemical weapons]."

The Arguments of the Progenitors of the Invasion of Iraq   17

    3. Iraq has a nuclear weapons programs. Powell states that all the evidence he will present is based on information supplied by defectors, such as the following:
        a. "Saddam Hussein had a massive clandestine nuclear-weapons program that covered several different techniques to enrich uranium."
        b. He told the IAEA that Iraq had no nuclear weapons program.
        c. "Saddam Hussein already possesses two out of the three key components needed to build a nuclear bomb . . . nuclear scientists . . . and a bomb design."
        d. "Saddam Hussein . . . has made repeated attempts . . . to acquire high-specification aluminum tubes from 11 different countries."
        e. "Iraq is attempting to acquire magnets and high-speed balancing machines. Both items can be used in a gas centrifuge program to enrich uranium."

    Powell again draws the exceedingly strong conclusion from this listing that on the basis of what he has presented, "there is no doubt" that "Saddam Hussein is very much focused on obtaining the technology needed to make nuclear weapons."

    4. Iraq is developing delivery systems to deliver weapons of mass destruction. Powell presents the following evidence:
        a. "Numerous intelligence reports from the past decade from sources inside Iraq indicate that Saddam Hussein retains a covert force of up to a few dozen Scud-variant ballistic missiles . . . with a range of 650 to 900 kilometers."
        b. Iraq admitted that it had al Samoud 2 missiles, which violate the 150 kilometer limit established by U.N. Resolution 687.
        c. UNMOVIC reported that Iraq has illegally imported 380 SA-2 rocket engines. "These are likely for use in the al Samoud 2."
        d. "One program is pursuing a liquid fuel missile that would be able to fly more than 1,200 kilometers."
        e. Iraq is developing unmanned aerial vehicles (UAV's). "There is ample evidence that Iraq has [been] testing spray devices" for the UAV's.
    5. Iraq is linked with terrorism. The evidence Powell presented:
        a. "Baghdad trains Palestine liberation Front members in small arms and explosives. Saddam used the Arab Liberation Front to funnel money to the families of Palestinian suicide bombers." No corroborating evidence was presented here.
        b. "Saddam's own intelligence service was involved in dozens of attacks or attempted assassinations in the 1990's." Again, no evidence presented.
        c. There is "a sinister nexus between Iraq and the Al Qaeda terrorist network . . . Iraq today harbors a deadly terrorist network, headed by Abu Musaab al-Zarqawi, an associate and collaborator of Osama bin Laden." Powell showed a picture of a camp, said it was in Northeastern Iraq, and called it Zarqawi's camp.

d. A senior Baghdad official offered Al Qaeda members from Afghanistan safe harbor in Iraq, and they accepted it. No evidence in support of this was offered by Mr. Powell.

e. "Iraqi officials deny these accusations . . . but they are not credible."

f. "An Al Qaeda source tells us that Saddam and bin Laden reached an understanding that al Qaeda would no longer support activities against Baghdad."

g. There were "secret Iraqi intelligence high-level contacts with al Qaeda. We know members of both organizations met repeatedly and have met at least eight times at very senior levels since the early 1990's."

h. "Saddam became more interested as he saw al Qaeda's appalling attacks" in 1998 and 2000.

i. "One of Saddam's former intelligence chiefs in Europe says Saddam sent his agents to Afghanistan sometime in the mid-1990's to provide training to al Qaeda members."

j. In response to those who say that "Saddam Hussein's secular tyranny and al Qaeda's religious tyranny do not mix[,] I am not comforted by this thought. Ambition and hatred are enough to bring Iraq and al Qaeda together.

k. Saddam is also involved with Hamas, which "opened an office in Baghdad in 1999, and Iraq has hosted conferences attended by Palestine Islamic Jihad."

l. "Iraq provided training in [weapons of mass destruction] to al Qaeda."

What are we to make of the remarkable series of accusations Colin Powell makes against Iraq and its alleged various nefarious deeds?

First, note the incredible *lack* of evidence Powell actually presents. While he makes many broadside attacks regarding the alleged notorious deeds of Saddam Hussein and Iraq, he rarely supports his accusations. Even when he makes appeals to witnesses, he does not name them or even tell how they might have had their stories verified.

Furthermore, Powell makes numerous logical errors. Even if we assume most of his evidence is accurate, he frequently draws the strongest conclusion possible, and his conclusions simply are not supported by the weight of the evidence. More than this, most of his conclusions are based on ignorance. For example, "there is no evidence that Saddam Hussein ceased his nuclear weapons program" turns into "Saddam Hussein is continuing his nuclear weapons program." The first statement does not imply the second.

Third, immediately after his presentation was concluded, there were some journalists who discovered some telling things about the information that Powell presented. First, much of it was a "cut and paste" job done from previously published academic articles that were based on dated material. For example, according to journalist John Nichols, "substantial portions of the report that Powell used to support his critique of Iraq were lifted from an article written by a postgraduate student who works not in Baghdad but in Monterey, California, and who based much of his research on materials left in Kuwait more than a dozen years ago by Iraqi security services." The student's name was Ibrahim al-Marashi. Further, "the content of six more pages . . . relies heavily on articles by Sean Boyne and Ken Gause that appeared in *Jane's Intelligence Review* in 1997 and 2002. None of these sources is acknowledged."[2]

Fourth, Hans Blix denied several of Powell's key claims. For example, Blix said UNMOVIC saw "no evidence" of mobile biological weapons labs, and "no persuasive indications" of Iraq-al Qaeda connections.[3] Further, UNMOVIC had no evidence of Iraq hiding and moving WMD materials. Again, CIA and FBI officials reported that there is no evidence for the Iraq-al Qaeda connection.[4]

Fifth, IAEA Director Mohammed El Baradei stated the opposite of what Powell claims: "There are no indications that there remains in Iraq any physical capability for the production of weapon-usable nuclear material of any practical significance," El Baradei wrote in a report to U.N. Secretary-General Kofi Annan.[5]

Regarding Powell's assertion that Iraq "may have" produced up to 25,000 liters of anthrax, the U.N. inspection agency said Iraq had destroyed its anthrax stocks at a known site. Iraq also presented a list of witnesses to verify that, but the war began before any witnesses on the list could be interviewed by the U.N.[6]

The video Powell played of the Iraqi F-1 Mirage jet spraying simulated anthrax was a video that predated the 1991 Persian Gulf war, when the Mirage was destroyed and three of the four spray tanks were destroyed.

Powell asserted that Iraq produced four tons of VX. However, most of it was destroyed in the 1990's under U.N. supervision. "Experts at Britain's International Institute of Strategic Studies said any pre-1991 VX most likely would have degraded anyway."[7]

The "aluminum tubes" accusation was shown to be a ruse, by the State Department intelligence bureau and the U.N.'s El Baradei, almost immediately after the accusation was made public.

So what of the other "hawks" who were advocating war with Iraq? Perhaps they did a better job at making the case for invasion than did the Bush administration.

The Public Arguments of the Supporters of Bush's War in Iraq

Peter Schwartz, writing for the Ayn Rand Institute, advocated a moral case for going to war with Iraq. After engaging in the usual accusations against Saddam Hussein (e.g. he is a dictator and he is brutal toward his people), Schwartz adds the assertion that Hussein had violated all 16 previous U.N. resolutions (we will show the falsehood of this statement below). Next, he claims that President Bush had been taking the diplomatic route with Hussein. But, says Schwartz, unless Mr. Bush takes the moral route, like Israel did with the destruction of Iraq's nuclear plant in 1981, his policy will fail. Why? Because the moral high ground, according to Schwartz, includes *not* seeking U.N. resolutions. It also recognizes that the U.S. would be fighting a defensive war, since Iraq posed a threat to the U.S. In addition, the other premises Schwartz adduces to support his pro-war conclusion are these:

> He [Saddam Hussein] went to war with us eleven years ago . . . He has chemical and biological weapons which can readily be delivered to the U.S. He is pursuing a program to acquire nuclear weapons. He finances and harbors terrorists.

From here, Schwartz draws his "moral" conclusion: "Any dictatorship that...attack[s] America's interests, is a threat that deserves to be eliminated. . . . The outlaw-state of Iraq has no right to its 'territorial integrity'."

Aside from the hysterical tone of the article, Schwartz's alleged "moral" argument is in fact not moral at all, based as it is completely on self-interest. Although it is a primary plank of the Rand philosophy that self-interest is the bane of moral behavior, there are few philosophers who would agree with this, since morality is defined almost universally as the examination our responsibilities toward others.[8] Even if a notion of "enlightened self-interest" made its way into general definitions of morality, the hard task would then be to determine precisely what is in the best interest of the U.S. in relation to Iraq. If Iraq is not a direct threat—and Mr. Schwartz perceives it to be just this—then there is no argument for self-interest possible that would support an invasion. But if Iraq in fact had the weapons to attack America, moral codes as well as international law would still require that the threat be imminent. Schwartz never bothers to make this case. Thus, even if all of Mr. Schwartz's premises were true, his conclusion, that if Mr. Bush takes the "moral route" he will win, is untenable. But Schwartz bases all his "facts" on U.S. government claims, claims that very many people were disputing, and he gives no references or credence to any other evidence.

William Safire, prominent *New York Times* columnist, fully supported the war. He laid out his arguments in a piece entitled "Clear Ties of Terror," in the January 27, 2003 edition of the *Times*. In it, Safire stated that his Kurdish sources had informed him that Saddam Hussein "has armed and financed a fifth column of Al Qaeda Mullahs and terrorists." Their assignment was "to assassinate the free Kurds who made up the only anti-Saddam leadership inside Iraq." In addition, Safire quoted President Bush's speech in Cincinnati from October, 2002: "some Al Qaeda leaders who fled Afghanistan went to Iraq." He was referring to Zarqawi. Case closed, for Safire. However, Safire ignores two crucial premises that overturn his argument. The first premise missing is the important fact that northern Iraq, where Zarqawi was alleged to be, was not in the control of Saddam Hussein. In addition, the Kurdish connection of Hussein to Al Qaeda was never verified and remained highly dubious prior to the invasion, for the very reasons that "did not comfort" Mr. Powell: bin Laden and Hussein were ideologically opposed, not just religiously, but politically. In April of 1998, bin Laden called Hussein an "infidel." In 2002, CIA intelligence showed that Hussein considered bin Laden an enemy of Iraq.[9] So Mr. Safire also failed to provide the evidence we need to justify an invasion of Iraq.

Kenneth Pollack, a former CIA analyst of the Iraq army, was also a supporter of the invasion. He wrote at least two articles in the *New York Times*, in September of 2002 and February 21, 2003, providing his pro-invasion arguments. In the first article, "Why Iraq Can't Be Deterred," Pollack states that the usual nuclear deterrence argument regarding nuclear nations (i.e. mutually assured destruction) will not work with Saddam Hussein, because "Mr. Hussein is often intentionally suicidal—that is, he miscalculates his odds of success and frequently ignores the likelihood of catastrophic failure." What Pollack ignores completely is that MAD is for nations that already possess nuclear weapons. The sense in which deterrence had been used with Saddam Hussein is that he is to be prevented from obtaining nuclear weapons. This definition of deterrence, quite different from the one to which Pollack refers, makes his argument unsound. *A fortiori*, it makes his conclusions that Hussein would use nuclear weapons to punish Israel and control the Mideast vacuous. Hussein could clearly be deterred from getting nuclear weapons, with the very tight inspections program the U.N. had engaged in Iraq. As numerous articles from former U.N. inspector Scott Ritter and Mohamed El Beradei have shown, the weapons inspection program in Iraq was working. We will detail these arguments and articles below.

Pollack's second article in the *Times* embracing the coming invasion of Iraq was written on February 21, 2003. Entitled "Last Chance to Stop Iraq," Pollack uses the same line that the Bush administration had been using: that stories from Iraq defectors indicate that Iraq was very close to developing a nuclear weapon. Because of the discrepancy between U.N. inspector reports and Iraqi defector reports, Pollack concludes that "we simply do not know how close Iraq is to acquiring a nuclear weapon . . . What we do know is that for more than a decade we have consistently overestimated the ability of inspectors to impede the Iraqi efforts and we have consistently underestimated how far along Iraq has been toward acquiring nuclear weapons." But using defectors as evidence is a little like using tortured prisoners: they will say whatever they think the other side wants to hear in order to get what they want. Pollack's reliance on unnamed and uncorroborated defector stories is an insufficient premise for him to use to conclude the dubious nature of the inspection process, let alone justify an invasion by U.S. military forces.

But Pollack is not finished with his argument. He adds that fear of retaliation is probably what kept Saddam Hussein from using chemical weapons against the coalition troops during the Gulf War of 1991, but that he did blow up the Kuwaiti oil fields and "tried to send terrorist teams to America" despite warning from Secretary of State James Baker that he would face "terrible consequences" if he did any of those three things.

No one doubts that Saddam Hussein was an abusive tyrant domestically, as well as a bad general who consistently miscalculated the moves of his enemies, and that nuclear weapons in his hands would not be a good thing. But that does not imply that an invasion and occupation of Iraq was a legitimate response to the uncertainties of deterrence. If international laws of war and ethics are to be violated simply for the reasons that a preferred course of action carries with it possible failure, then there is no structure of international relations that can be relied upon to begin with, and nuclear war becomes inevitable. Article 51 of the U.N. Charter obliges nations to withhold military aggression except in the face of imminent attack from another nation. Further, Pollack relies on counterfactuals for this segment of his argument, and the "what if" scenarios he constructs, while certainly worth considering, could in the end be used to justify nearly any military invasion of one country against another.

Pollack's final argument is based on both dubious and flatly false premises. First of all, he states that "all the evidence" indicates that Saddam believed that he would be in for a fight from the U.S. if he invaded Kuwait. But all of the evidence that Pollack proffers only allows us to conclude that Saddam Hussein wanted to be the dominating power in the Middle East. It does not allow him to conclude that an invasion in 2003 was the only way to deter him from accomplishing his goal. The argument is a non-sequitur.

His flatly false premise occurs when he states that "only Saddam Hussein sees these [nuclear] weapons as offensive—as enabling aggression." Pollack has completely ignored the fact that Mr. Bush, in 2002, made public the plans of his administration not only for U.S. first use of nuclear weapons, but for use on terrorists, bunkers, and munitions of perceived enemies.

So we are still in search of a "smoking gun" argument to legitimate the Iraq invasion of 2003 by the U.S. that allows it to override international law and the will of the world. Julia Preston hoped to fill that lacuna when she reported that Hans Blix, one of the chief U.N. inspectors in Iraq, filed a 15-page report concluding that Iraq had failed to prove that they have eliminated illegal weapons.[11] Preston quotes the Blix report as stating that there are "indications" that Iraq had created weapons using VX; that Iraq provided contradictory information in its 12,200-page report to the U.N.; that Iraq failed to account for 6,500 chemical bombs, and other allegations that we have already seen in Mr. Powell's U.N. address. We also knew at the time that such assessments were based on dated evidence, but Preston does not add that in her article.

Note the tone of Preston's article: Iraq hasn't proven they have stopped their programs, so we can conclude that they are still engaged in them. Aside from the illogical conclusion (absence of evidence proves nothing except in a court of law), the Blix report does not say this at all. In fact, Blix took pains to make it clear that there is no evidence that Iraq had reconstituted its nuclear program. Dr. El Baradei, the director of the IAEA (International Atomic Energy Agency) confirmed Blix's assertion, stating in his report that satellite photography showed no new nuclear activities being undertaken.

In March, Anne-Marie Slaughter, the dean of the Woodrow Wilson School of Public and International Affairs at Princeton University, added to the beating of the war drums by arguing in the *Times* that there are "Good Reasons for Going Around the U.N." in order to war with Iraq. Her reasons: the fact that the U.S. has done it before, with Kosovo, and that if the Iraqi people welcome the coming of the U.S. as liberators and the U.S. turns immediately back to the U.N. for rebuilding Iraq.[12] She adds that the U.N. "cannot be a straightjacket, preventing nations from defending themselves or pursuing what they perceive to be in their vital national security interests." Ms. Slaughter concludes "that which is legitimate is also legal." But this is a non-sequitur argument, as Ms. Slaughter completely ignored international law in this argument, which would clearly see the invasion as illegal. Significantly, she disregarded the Kellogg-Briand Pact of 1928, to which the U.S. was a signatory. This Act rejected recourse to war as an instrument of foreign policy. Additionally, she ignored the Nuremberg Charter, Article 6, which makes criminal invasions of other countries as "Crimes against Peace," and the United Nations Charter, Articles 2(3), 2(4), and 51, all of which condemn the use of force against another nation without imminent provocation. Stated philosophically, Ms. Slaughter places a perceived national interest above the law, which is a dubious contention, and certainly not a *casus belli*. But her weakest premise is her first one, arguing that historical precedent makes for legality. That same premise would legitimate Hitler's invasion of France, once he had invaded other countries.

Since many of the arguments favoring the invasion of Iraq in 2003 have been based on United Nations reports and resolutions, perhaps now is the time to examine those U.N. documents. We will begin with a few of the U.N. resolutions pertaining to Iraq which bear particular importance to the U.S. invasion.

The United Nations on Iraq

United Nations resolutions concerning Iraq began in August of 1990, with UNSCR 660 and 661. These resolutions condemned the invasion of Kuwait by Iraq and imposed economic sanctions on the latter country. Since then, there have been at least eleven further resolutions concerning Iraq (687, 688, 706, 707, 949, 986, 1051, 1137, 1284, 1409, and 1441). For our purposes, it is important only to examine resolutions 687 and 1441, both of which were written by the United States.

Resolution 687, dated April 3, 1991, called for the destruction, removal or neutralizing of all chemical and biological weapons, and cessation of all research and development for ballistic missiles which had a range over 150 km. It also created a special commission to inspect Iraq compliance with this resolution (UNSCOM).

Resolution 1441, adopted November 8, 2002, "decides that Iraq has been and remains in material breach of its obligations under relevant resolutions...decides to set up an enhanced inspection regime...decides that Iraq shall provide UNMOVIC and the IAEA immediate, unimpeded, unconditional, and unrestricted access to any and all, including underground, areas, facilities, buildings, equipment, records, and means of transport which they wish to inspect," among other declarations.

It is under these two resolutions that the International Atomic Energy Agency (IAEA) and the United Nations Monitoring, Verification and Inspection Commission (UNMOVIC) were formed. Their work in inspecting the weapons situation in Iraq was to determine whether or not the coalition led by the U.S. would strike that country. Their reports, dated January and February, 2003, respectively, were the pretext used by the U.S. to invade and occupy Iraq.

The problem for the U.S. was that the IAEA report was generally positive regarding the cooperation Iraq was giving concerning its nuclear weapons programs. The IAEA report stated that "there were no indications to suggest that Iraq had been successful in its attempt to produce nuclear weapons," and that "all nuclear material of significance to Iraq's nuclear weapons programme was verified and fully accounted for." This report went largely unnoticed by the U.S. media. They wanted a more condemnatory report on Iraq, and they got it in the form of the UNMOVIC report and in the report of the chief weapons inspector for UNMOVIC, Hans Blix.

The UNMOVIC report was a mix of statements of Iraqi violations and also Iraqi compliances with U.N. Resolutions 687 and 1441. Iraqi violations included the following:

- The December 7, 2002 Iraqi Declaration presented to UNMOVIC, totaling 12,200 pages, provided dated facts and not "much new supporting documentation or other evidence. This includes the part that covered Iraq's biological weapons, chemical weapons, and missile delivery systems.
- When UNMOVIC exercised its right, under UNSCR 1441, to interview Iraqi officials involved in weapons programs, all 28 of them refused. Prior to the next round of discussions with the government, some were changing their minds and becoming open to the interviews, under "encouragement" from the Iraqi government. The war began before UNMOVIC was able to conduct those interviews.
- Iraq's surface-to-surface missiles were capable of passing the 150km distance limitation set by UNSCR 687.
- The "casting chambers" in which Iraq could produce motors for missiles, destroyed during the 1991 Gulf War, were refurbished by Iraq, in violation of 687.
- The list of all personnel involved in Iraq's weapons program, required of Iraq under 1441, was deemed inadequate by UNMOVIC.

While the mainstream U.S. media made much of this report, it unfairly ignored the record of Iraqi compliance and changes in the attitudes of Iraqi officials regarding compliance.[13] Here is also what the UNMOVIC report stated regarding Iraqi compliance and changes:

- The chemical weapons report and the missile delivery systems report from Iraq contained new information of which inspectors were not previously aware.
- Of the over 200 chemical and over 100 biological samples that were analyzed by UNMOVIC, nearly all of them were shown to be "consistent with Iraq's declarations."
- After negotiations, the Iraq government permitted use of aerial surveillance and ensured the safety of those surveillance aircraft, such as the U-2 spy plane of the U.S.

- Even though the original list of those involved in the Iraqi weapons program was deemed to be inadequate by UNMOVIC, Iraq eventually did produce a full listing.
- The empty 122-mm chemical munitions, made by the U.S. media into a casus belli, were tagged for destruction.
- Iraq appointed its own commission for undertaking comprehensive searches for more such munitions, and found six more outside of the inspections done by UNMOVIC. These were reported to UNMOVIC.
- Iraq informed UNMOVIC of two complete and 118 remnants of aerial bombs it had discovered.

In conclusion, UNMOVIC has reported that, "in general, Iraq has been helpful on 'process,' meaning, first of all, that Iraq has from the outset satisfied the demand for prompt access to any site, whether or not it had been previously declared or inspected." Furthermore, "after some initial difficulties" in several areas of UNMOVIC concern, such as escorting flights into the no-fly Zone, and surveillance aircraft over Iraq, the Iraqis cooperated with UNMOVIC demands. The report concluded that "even with the requisite cooperation [from Iraq], [disarmament and verification] will inevitably require some time."

Thus, while it is true that Iraq resisted the U.N. inspectors, and indeed played "cat and mouse" as a result, and while it is true that they had violated some terms of UNSCR 687 and 1441, the cooperation was proceeding apace. Inspections were working. That this is indeed the case was made clear in the report made by chief U.N. weapons inspector Hans Blix. Although Blix was slightly more damning in his assessment of Iraqi cooperation and compliance (and no doubt for this reason his report was seized upon by the U.S. media over the UNMOVIC general report), Blix, too maintained that things were progressing in Iraq: "UNMOVIC, for its part, is not presuming that there are proscribed items and activities in Iraq, but nor is it . . . presuming the opposite." The Blix report made some of the same complaints that the UNMOVIC general report did, while also asserting Iraqi cooperation in many areas of concern. He refused to be pessimistic or optimistic, but held that there could be trust-building that could be developed with more inspections.

Hardly any of this made it to the front page news of the media. One brief example of media condemnation of Iraq on the basis of the Blix report alone was mentioned above in the reporting of Julia Preston for the *New York Times*. Nearly every major media outlet participated in the same one-sided reporting that contributed to the efforts of the Bush administration to invade Iraq. However, not everyone was silent nor was every media outlet complicit. Here are some examples of arguments that were made opposing the invasion and occupation, prior to March 19, 2003, the day it began.

Notes

1. All charges listed here, unless otherwise noted, were taken from the U.S. Department of State web site on February 27, 2003.
2. John Nichols, "Dubious Dossier," *The Nation*, February 7, 2003.
3. Phyllis Bennis, "Powell's U.N. Presentation," *The Nation*, February 17, 2003.
4. Neil Mackay, "Why the CIA Thinks Bush is Wrong," *The Sunday Herald* (Scotland), October 13, 2002.
5. *Washington Times*, September 27, 2002.
6. U.N. News Centre, "Blix Welcomes Accelerated Cooperation by Iraq, but Says Unresolved Issues Remain," www.un.org, March 7, 2003.
7. Scott Ritter and William Rivers Pitt, War in Iraq (London: Profile Books, 2002).
8. For just a single example, see the popular ethics text by Louis Pojman, *Ethics: Discovering Right and Wrong*, in which Pojman defines ethics as seeking "to establish principles of right behavior that may serve as action guides for individuals and groups" (Belmont, California: Wadsworth, 1990), p. 2. For similar definitions, see, for example, Hugh Mercer Cutler, *Ethical Argument* (New York: Oxford University Press, 2004), p. 60, and Barbara McKinnon, *Ethics* (Belmont, California: Wadsworth, 2004), p. 3.
9. Walter Pincus, "CIA Learned in '02 That Bin Laden Had No Iraq Ties, Report Says," *Washington Post*, September 15, 2005.
10. Robert Parry, "Bush's Nuclear Gamble," Consortium News, September 30, 2002.
11. Julia Preston, "Inspector Says Iraq Falls Short," *New York Times*, January 28, 2003.
12. Anne-Marie Slaughter, "Good Reasons for Going around the U.N." *New York Times*, March, 18, 2003.
13. For more on the lopsided media coverage being given to the Iraq issue during the run-up to the invasion, see the publications by Fairness and Accuracy in Reporting (FAIR) at www.fair.org.

Chapter Three
Refutation of the Arguments Supporting the Invasion

In a *New York Times* article entitled "Experts Warn of High Risk for American Invasion of Iraq," dated August 1, 2002, James Dao reported that former senior military officers and nongovernment experts on Iraq presented to a Senate committee their doubts about the easy outcome of a possible invasion. Dao states that in that hearing "there was a broad consensus among the varied experts that if President Bush decided to use military force to remove Mr. Hussein . . . the Pentagon could not assume that the Iraqi military . . . would carry on the fight alone . . . [and] the administration should plan on keeping forces in Iraq for many years to help rebuild it."

William O. Beeman, in a February 6, 2003 column in the *Pacific News Service*, argued in an article, "Al Qaeda-Iraq Connection Tenuous at Best," that the only connection Bush could make was with al-Zarqawi, and there "has been no information revealed that would show that al-Zarqawi ever met with Iraqi officials." Nor is there any evidence supporting the administration's assertions "that al-Zarqawi runs a terrorist network of his own or that he is the No. 3 figure in al Qaeda."

Nicholas D. Kristof argued for the continuation of the Eisenhower—Kennedy—Reagan policies of "containment" rather than invasion (regarding, respectively, Egypt, Cuba, and Libya).[1] Michael Walzer, political scientist at Princeton, agreed, arguing that we should keep "the little war" of no-fly zones and inspection of imports, going. This would be done, according to Walzer, by expanding the northern and southern no-fly zones; by imposing "smart sanctions;" by the U.S. imposing unilateral sanctions on countries that violated U.N. sanctions on Iraq; that the U.N. monitoring system on Iraq be expanded; and challenge the French to send troops, since they want to hold for a "last resort" before warring with Iraq again.[2]

The *New York Times* staff editorial of March 9 was entitled "Saying No to War." In it, they argued that "the report of the inspectors . . . was generally devastating to the American position. They not only argued that progress was being made, they also discounted the idea that Iraq was actively attempting to manufacture nuclear weapons." Regarding Iraq harboring terrorists, another Bush excuse for invasion, the *Times* stated "that same accusation could be lodged against any number of American allies in the region . . . nations are not supposed to launch military invasions based on hunches and fragmentary evidence." Regarding Mr. Bush's argument that Iraq refuses to disarm, the *Times* stated that this reason was insufficient, since "the U.N. itself believes disarmament is occurring and the weapons inspections can be made to work." Furthermore, importing democracy cannot be the U.S. goal when there is no broad international consensus on doing this with Iraq. Finally, the *Times* argued that the U.S. needs "to demonstrate by example that there are certain rules that everybody has to follow, one of the most important of which is that you do not invade another country for any but the most compelling of reasons."

Perhaps of all the anti-invasion articles written, former president Jimmy Carter came the closest to the philosophical theory of the "Just War" principles, by actually using the principles in his analysis.[3] The "last resort" criterion, Carter argued, had not been met by the Bush administration, because the other options were outlined by the U.N. Security Council and our own leaders (although Carter does not specify what he has in mind in making these references). Further, Mr. Carter states that "the war's weapons must discriminate between combatants and noncombatants. . . . General Tommy R. Franks, commander of American troops in the Persian Gulf, has expressed concern about many of the military targets being near hospitals, schools, mosques and private homes." Third, Mr. Carter rightly states that the violence of the war must be proportional to the injury we have received. Yet the case connecting Iraq to 9/11 is, in Mr. Carter's word, "unconvincing." Nor do we have international authority to occupy Iraq for over a decade in order to bring *Pax Americana* to the region. Thus, the requirement of rightful authority is unmet. Finally, Carter states that the peace the war establishes "must be a clear improvement over what exists." But destabilizing the region and prompting terrorists to further jeopardize our security at home is not a better peace. In addition, by defying the U.N., the U.S. will undermine it as a viable institution for world peace.

So the voices of opposition were strong and weighty, if unnoticed and unacknowledged in the U.S. headlong rush to war. But since Mr. Carter introduced the requirements of Just War thinking into the discussion, now is the time for us to perform a more extensive philosophical analysis of the Bush invasion of Iraq. Can the invasion and subsequent occupation of Iraq be justified on terms of the Justified War Tradition?

The Just War Theory and Iraq: Pro and Con Arguments Concerning the Invasion

The first thing that even a casual observer of the public pre-invasion debate on Iraq had to notice was the stark paucity of discussion about moral principles and international law, particularly from those who supported the invasion. That dearth was not met by a similar one from the intellectual community. Many of the articles written by intellectuals using the Just War Theory were in fact skeptical of the morality of what the Bush administration had proposed concerning Iraq. But not all intellectuals were opposed to the coming invasion. One of the more spirited defenses of the Bush proposal concerning Iraq came from Thomas M. Nichols, Chairman of the Department of Strategy and Policy at the U.S. Naval War College. John Langan, S.J., professor of Catholic Social Thought at Georgetown University, while skeptical of the possibility of putting a moral face on the invasion, nonetheless argued that many of the goals that the Bush administration used in defense of the invasion were morally acceptable. In this mix is the position taken by the author and literary critic Christopher Hitchens, a regular contributor to neocon publications such as *The Weekly Standard*. Since Hitchens offers evidence and arguments that the intellectuals who supported the invasion did not, we will use Hitchens to bolster the pro-war case somewhat as we examine this position.

The centuries-old structure around which justified wars were debated is a series of individually necessary and jointly sufficient conditions for going to war and also for one's conduct in war that, taken together, is called "The Just War Theory." While there are various problems that have been raised concerning some of these criteria, they generally suffice for a thorough examination of the ethics and legality of going to war. In fact, notable requirements of the international laws of war are predicated on Just War Theory principles. Just War Theory requires that each of these conditions be met before declaring that engaging in war is ethically justified.

Just Cause

John Langan quite correctly says that "[i]n the absence of a just cause, there can be no just war; so this will always be the most fundamental requirement."[4] It is also here where the Bush administration case for going to war with Iraq will either stand or fall.

The Pro-Invasion Argument Concerning Just Cause

Unfortunately, President Bush and the members of his administration have equivocated and vacillated on the cause of the invasion. It was sometimes said to have been for the alleged possession and development by Iraq of weapons of mass destruction, forbidden by UNSCR 687 and 1441.[5] At other times it was for the purpose of "regime change;" at still other times it was for the connections alleged between Saddam Hussein and the events of 9/11/01 in the U.S.;[6] still again it was for the alleged Iraq-al Qaeda connection;[7] and finally for "spreading democracy in the Middle East."

Those writers who supported the invasion were quick to attempt to put some flesh on the bones of these causes. Thomas M. Nichols, in an article published in *Ethics & International Affairs*, crafted the listing of events to support the Bush rationale that the cause was just for military action against Iraq:

> Iraq has shown itself to be a serial aggressor led by a dictator willing to run imprudent risks, including an attack on the civilians of a noncombatant nation during the Persian Gulf War; a supreme enemy of human rights that has already used weapons of mass destruction against civilians; a consistent violator of both U.N. resolutions and the terms of the 1991 cease-fire treaty, to say nothing of the laws of armed conflict and the Geneva Conventions before and since the Persian Gulf War; a terrorist entity that has attempted to reach beyond its own borders to support and engage in illegal activities that have included the attempted assassination of a former U.S. president; and most important, a state that has relentlessly sought nuclear arms against all international demands that it cease such efforts.[8]

The conclusion Nichols draws from this impressive list of Saddam Hussein crimes is that "*any one* of these would be sufficient to remove Saddam and his regime . . . but taken together they are brief for what can only be considered a just war" (emphasis added).

Adding to the just cause, for Nichols, is the fact that Saddam had not only "repeatedly" violated the 1991 cease-fire agreement (i.e. UNSCR 687), but done so in "blatant and contemptuous" fashion. Nichols does not elaborate on what these "contemptuous" violations were. He merely asserts that "violation of a cease-fire treaty has long been accepted as one of the clearest moments allowing the renewal of hostilities."

Nichols further classifies Iraq's "repeated acts of aggression:" not accepting the no-fly zones and firing on over 700 U.S. flights over the zones, and attempting to assassinate former President George H.W. Bush.

As the article continues, Nichols becomes more and more vitriolic and less and less balanced in his argument. He concludes by stating that the only two choices we face are to invade Iraq or let Saddam "command an arsenal of the most deadly materials on earth . . . there is no third choice."

Not to be outdone, Christopher Hitchens adds his own evidence to the justice of the cause of going to war with Iraq, by compiling the following list of Saddam crimes: he "committed genocide on [Iraq's] own soil, harbored and nurtured international thugs and killers, and flouted every provision of the Non-Proliferation Treaty. . . . Meanwhile, every species of gangster from the hero of the Achille Lauro hijacking to Abu Musab al Zarqawi was finding hospitality under Saddam's crumbling roof."[9]

In addition, Hitchens proffers the following evidence supporting Iraq's weapons of mass destruction program: Abdul Rahman Yasin, "who mixed the chemicals for the World Trade Center attack in 1993, subsequently found refuge in Baghdad; that Dr. Mahdi Obeidi, Saddam's senior physicist, was able to lead American soldiers to nuclear centrifuge parts and a blueprint for a complete centrifuge . . . that Saddam's agents were in Damascus as late as February 2003, negotiating to purchase missiles off the shelf from North Korea...that Rolf Ekeus, the great Swedish socialist . . . was offered a $2 million bribe in a face-to-face meeting with Tariq Aziz."

One can also find, as part of the case for war made by Hitchens, an interesting argument that the U.S. must invade Iraq as a humanitarian intervention. The reason is because that country has been shredded by "three decades of war and fascism" (he conveniently neglects to mention twelve years of economic sanctions, led by the U.S.), such that the conclusion must be that "in logic and morality, one must therefore compare the current state of the country with the likely or probable state of it" if the U.S. does not invade. "All of the alternatives would have been infinitely worse," asserts Hitchens, as he goes on to paint a doomsday scenario in which Turkey, Iran, and Saudi Arabia invade Iraq to stop Saddam Hussein, followed by an American intervention to clean up, after "a more costly and bloody intervention" than the one planned by Bush.

Analysis of the Pro Argument on Just Cause

Response to Claims of Bush Administration. That the Bush administration distorted information on Iraq's WMD's has been dealt with above in the section on U.N. reports. But by way of summary, we can state that Hans Blix, head of the UNMOVIC, stated to the UNSC on January 9, 2003 that "if we had found any 'smoking gun' we would have reported it to the Council. . . . We have not submitted any such reports."[10] Dr. Mohamed El Baradei, director of the International Atomic Energy Agency (IAEA) reported that they had uncovered "no evidence of ongoing . . . nuclear activities."[11] A study issued by the University of Notre Dame on February 6, 2003 (six weeks before the invasion) states that there is overwhelming evidence presented to by UNSCOM that Iraq had in fact destroyed most of its chemical and biological agents in the 1990's.[12] The report concluded that "[i]n the last two months U.N. monitors have conducted more than 300 inspections of possible chemical, biological and missile sites in Iraq and have found no evidence or documentation confirming the existence of the alleged chemical and biological stockpiles."[13]

Regarding the alleged link between Iraq and al Qaeda, or Iraq and 9/11/01, the U.S. State Department, the CIA, the FBI, and the Pakistani intelligence agency all reported that there was no evidence of a link between Iraq and al Qaeda. On May 2, 2002, "FBI Director Robert Mueller said that, after an exhaustive FBI and CIA investigation, no direct link has been found between Iraq and any of the September 11 hijackers."[14]

Response to Claims of Nichols. The list of studies from the United Nations, the U.S. State Department, the CIA, the FBI, and other agencies should be enough to demonstrate clearly that the claims Nichols makes are very broad and general in the first instance ("a terrorist entity that has attempted to reach beyond its own borders to support and engage in illegal activities;"), untrue statements in other instances ("relentlessly sought nuclear arms against all international demands that it cease such efforts;" "a consistent violator of both U.N. resolutions and the terms of the 1991 cease-fire treaty"), insufficient in law or morality to launch a preemptive attack on another nation (the "attack on the civilians of a noncombatant nation during the Persian Gulf War" and that he "has already used weapons of mass destruction against civilians." Both happened during the Gulf War of 1991, and are not legitimate pretexts for a 2003 invasion. This would be the moral equivalent of double jeopardy). Nichols is also incorrect to assert that "*any one* of these would be sufficient to remove Saddam and his regime . . . but taken together they are brief for what can only be considered a just war." In fact, none of them by itself is a sufficient condition for a preemptive war, if that in fact is what the U.S. was attempting to do. We will support and examine this assertion in more detail below. For now, it will suffice to say that none of these issues taken singly allows for a definition of "imminent threat" to be fulfilled. It is this imminence of military action that allows for an invasion, both morally and legally. Perhaps worst of all, he commits the logical fallacy of false dilemma when he argues that the only options we face are invade Iraq or let Saddam have WMD's and use them. There are quite obviously other routes to take short of military action. The inspections were certainly working, as demonstrated by the conclusion Dr. Blix made in January, 2003, that the "more weapons of mass destruction were destroyed under [the disarmament process] than were destroyed during the Gulf War." That is strong evidence that there is a workable and working alternative to Nichols' argument for invasion.

Response to Claims of Hitchens. First off all, let us make a point in logic for Mr. Hutchins. Assuming the veracity of his evidence, it is still not enough to make the case for invasion of another country when the United States is not directly or imminently threatened. His examples are only circumstantial, and although they might be persuasive on Court TV, they are insufficient in law or morality to make the case to invade and occupy another country. He accuses Saddam of harboring "every species of gangster from the hero of the Achille Lauro hijacking to Abu Musab al Zarqawi," then presents only one case to support it. This is a clear example of a hasty generalization. Even if he had added the names of the two terrorists William Safire alleges Saddam was giving safe harbor, it is still not enough to state that invasion is the proper response. Justified Cause for a full scale war requires imminent threat of military invasion by another country, not the fact that a country harbors a few known terrorists.

Just as critical as all of this, the evidence Hitchens provides is false. For example, Kenneth Pollack, who at the time worked in the State Department, stated that there was no CIA information tying Adbul Rahman Yasin, one of the "terrorists" Hitchens uses as a *casus belli*, to the 1993 World Trade Center bombing. Again, in May of 2002, on the CBS program "60 Minutes," Leslie Stahl interviewed him from an Iraqi prison and found him in handcuffs and prison clothes.

Furthermore, on the news program "Democracy Now!" of September 16, 2003, it was reported that Iraq had attempted to hand Yasin over to the U.S. in exchange for a lifting of sanctions. The U.S. refused to negotiate.

Hitchens uses the statements of Rolf Ekeus, former executive chairman of UNSCOM on Iraq from 1991-1997, as evidence to war with Iraq. But Ekeus interviewed General Hussein Kamel, Saddam Hussein's son-in-law, in 1995, who testified that "all weapons, biological, chemical, missile, nuclear, were destroyed."[15]

Finally, the implied humanitarian intervention in the argument Hitchens uses to support a U.S. invasion is a red herring. First, Saddam Hussein in 2003 was not involved—and had not been involved for the previous decade—in cleansing his citizens. The only possible exception to this would be the Kurds, and since they had a relatively safe haven in the northern "no-fly zone" of Iraq, he could not get to them easily, and has not done so to any significant degree. So although Saddam was a brutal dictator, the ethnic cleansing that would justify an American humanitarian invasion was not part of the current crimes which he had been accused of committing.

Given the flimsy evidence and the lack of logic that went into Hitchens' argument, it is safe to say that Hitchens reached his conclusion first, then "grasped at straws" to find the evidence to support it. This is how we defined "deception" at the beginning of our study.[16] At best, his method is based on premises of U.S. unilateralism and self-interestedness, and it follows the pragmatic/utilitarian method without adding a sustained moral or legal analysis. It appears as though the Bush administration did the same thing.

The Method of the Pro-invasion Arguments. Note that neither Nichols nor Hitchens makes one reference to Just War Theory, international laws of aggression, nor to general moral principles and arguments. Both writers argue strictly from the pragmatic perspective, and conclude that the invasion is legitimate from that utilitarian point of view. For them, if the consequences will be good and the man to be deposed bad, then the just cause criterion is satisfied for them. This is especially true for Hitchens, who lists all the "positive accounting" of the invasion, and justifies it on the grounds of the good consequences to come from it. But pragmatic argument does not make for a moral argument, and a moral argument must use normative principles to determine if an invasion is to be "justified." In fact, the pragmatic method of analyzing an event and its conceivable consequences undermines all moral arguments by disregarding them, replacing them with a utilitarian method. We want to know whether what we are doing as a nation is "right," and "right" cannot be determined without a sustained analysis of values and principles, such as Just War Theory provides. This is frequently accomplished by adopting a principle of universality, such as that suggested by Immanuel Kant. Kant, and others who follow his lead today, claim that a moral claim is a distinctively universal one, in that whatever I am willing to permit myself to do, I must permit everyone to do.[17] An unambiguous example of this moral concern may be demonstrated by distinguishing between preventive and preemptive wars. The former wars require imminent threat on the part of the nation to be attacked, whereas the latter simply attack a nation that someday might conceivably be a threat to another. The moral principle of universality would embrace the first distinction but not the second.

The Value Assumptions of the Pro-war Arguments. What is assumed in the arguments of Nichols and Hitchens is that a certain number of instances of bad international behavior on the part of the leader of a nation justifies an invasion of that nation. But does it? Not without adding a value/normative premise. Hitchens piling on particular instances in no way allows him to logically reach his value conclusion concerning the justifiability of the invasion of Iraq without this assumed value premise. Hitchens claims no more than that his premises are jointly sufficient conditions for the conclusion. But he needs to add the normative premise that "*many* violations of international law or U.N. mandates morally justify an invasion of Iraq."

Similarly, Nichols states explicitly that "any one of" the premises listing Saddam Hussein's bad behavior is a sufficient condition for invading Iraq. But is it? Again, this cannot be true without the value premise that "*any* violation of international law or U.N. mandates morally justifies an invasion of Iraq."

The question for each of these authors is whether or not, assuming their premises to be true, they provide moral justification for action from a collective representative body of the world, or whether they are justification for U.S. initiated and nearly-unilateral action. Neither author addresses this issue, although the context of their respective arguments seems to indicate that they are referring to unilateral U.S. action.

However, if this is true, then their cases are each weak, for they have to add a further premise concerning the moral legitimacy of unilateral action on the part of a nation that has not been attacked and is not under imminent threat. This would be a hard case for them to make, since it would in essence reject the criteria of both the traditional just war theory as well as international law concerning war. Thus, the stronger argument is to assume that they are referring to action on the part of the world collective (e.g. U.N.).

In view of all of this, let us reconstruct their respective arguments. For Nichols, each of Saddam's violations of international law and U.N. decrees constitutes a sufficient condition for the world to respond by going to war. Thus, according to Nichols' argument, the fact that Hussein has done this even once is sufficient moral cause for war. For Hitchens, the total amount of Hussein's violations legitimates a confrontational response from the world, and the fact that this has happened repeatedly is moral justification for war.

What can we make of these arguments? We have already demonstrated that most of the violations Nichols presents are not individually necessary conditions for legitimizing the invasion. Thus, his argument does not logically do what he claims it does.

That the premises are likewise not jointly sufficient, for either Nichols or Hitchens, can be shown by the ethical criteria of universality. This requires that we attempt to universalize our principles to see how well they fit our own situations. When attempting to make an argument concerning what we "ought" to do, what counts is the normative point of view. According to the German philosopher Jurgen Habermas, "a norm is just only if all can will that it be obeyed by each in comparable situations." In other words, the outcome of moral argumentation "turns on arguments showing that the interests embodied in contested norms are unreservedly universalizable."[18] One way of testing the universality of our norms is to see if each situation conceived allows one to maintain the same principle. Thus, if we can place our selves into a similar situation and consistently maintain the norm we espouse, we have a legitimate moral argument. If not, then the proposed action is not just and cannot morally be engaged.

The value premise in Hitchens' argument is vague, and in Nichols' argument is absurd. Nichols' normative premise is absurd because, if true, then any country may be invaded for a single violation of law or U.N. mandate. Without weighting values from innocent violations to gross violations, his conclusion is a *non sequitur*. So let us add this further assumption for Nichols: any generally recognized or agreed upon significant violation of international law is a pretext for invasion by the world collective. This remains absurd as a normative principle, for then it is still the case that numerous countries may invade other countries for singular acts, such as violation of a U.N. mandate.

Surely this is not what Nichols wants. If it is, then we should have invaded Israel, for instance, before we invaded Iraq, since Israel has ignored far more U.N. mandates concerning its nuclear weapons and its treatment of the Palestinians than has Iraq concerning weapons pursuits.

The argument Hitchens makes, with the use of jointly sufficient premises and a weaker moral principle, is a stronger argument. Still, though, when the criterion of universality is applied, it results in consequences unacceptable to the argument Hitchens is making. In other words, if a certain number of violations of international law or mandate is sufficient for invasion by the world, it is sufficient for any nation to be susceptible to intervention upon reaching a(n unknown) critical mass of violations. This application of the principle of normative universality opens the U.S. to precisely such attacks. The argument both authors present implies that we must allow other nations to attack the United States, for the U.S. has violated not just one, but many world mandates. They cannot all be detailed here, but for a sampling, we may state the following instances.

The Central American terrorist Luis Posada Carilles resides comfortably in Miami, Florida, after blowing up a Cuban plane carrying 72 passengers and also engaging in illegal work for the U.S. government in El Salvador. President George H.W. Bush pardoned Orlando Bosch, another terrorist who worked with the U.S. government.[19] In addition, the Bush administration, in direct violation of the Nuclear Proliferation Treaty, is arming India with nuclear weapons. The United States has also ignored the judgments of the World Court concerning its actions in Nicaragua, and has consistently rejected international law and claimed for itself alone the use of unilateral military attacks. Examples of this come from both the Bush and Clinton administrations.[20]

Applying the principle of universality as it must be applied to moral argumentation, these actions on the part of the United States are equal in importance to Saddam Hussein's starting wars and allegedly harboring terrorists. But neither Nichols nor Hitchens would allow the conclusion that the Central American countries are justified in invading and occupying the U.S. So their moral arguments each fail the test of universality of moral norms, and may be safely rejected.

A more cynical response would reject the universality requirement of normative arguments and appeal instead to the Thucydidian principle "the strong do as they can." But it is important to keep in mind that Hitchens and Nichols and others were attempting to make the *moral* case for invading Iraq.

Assuming that both authors were able to extricate themselves from the logical and moral problems we have just discussed, there is still a question to be asked concerning the legitimacy of reaching the conclusion that an invasion is morally justified and yet finding that other, more imperative moral reasons argue against such an action. For example, is respecting national sovereignty more important, as moral values go, than invading a country for past and possible future offenses? This is the hard question that is not asked by either author. Again, when is it the prerogative of one nation, with a few minor allies, to punish another nation which did not harm it or any current ally?

As to the factual nature of their individual premises, we may make the following observations.

First, Nichols implies that Iraq's attack on Israel and/or Iran is sufficient as a *casus belli*. In response, one must first note that these attacks occurred over a decade ago, and no longer serve for the justified cause Nichols wants. The attacks must be imminent, not long past, to serve as legitimate criteria for invasion. However, should Nichols insist on using historical premises, consistency requires that he argue that Israel be invaded by the U.S. on the same grounds, given their 1981 attack on Iraq's Osirak nuclear power plant, and their continuing attack on the civilian population of Palestine and the Gaza Strip.

Next, Nichols cites Hussein's attempt "to reach beyond his own borders" to engage in illegal activities, including attempted assassination (of former President Bush). Noam Chomsky presents the appropriate rebuttal, with his detailing of United States actions and assassinations in Central America.[21] Again, the appropriate conclusion is that Nichols' argument allows Central America to invade the U.S. Chomsky proceeds to demonstrate Israel's violations of numerous U.N. mandates as well, that Nichols ignores, including that "most important" premise to Nichols, the "attempt" to gain nuclear weapons. Israel already possesses them, in violation of U.N. 687, Article 14.

Hitchens argues that the invasion of Iraq is justified on humanitarian grounds, due to Iraq having committed genocide over a decade earlier and also being "shredded" by 12 years of war under Saddam. But humanitarian intervention is called for at the time it is needed, not 12 years after it happened. This makes his argument post hoc and thus irrelevant to the issue of a 2003 invasion. Even Michael Walzer, who allows for unilateral humanitarian interventions by a single nation, states the need for a "threat" that a people will be massacred.[22] The examples Walzer adduces—Cuba in 1898 and Bangladesh in 1971—indicate immediate unilateral responses of another nation—the U.S. and India, respectively, in Walzer's cases—to the initiation of a massacre of citizens. Applying this to the situation in Iraq, if Saddam Hussein actually had begun another round of massacres of his people, there would be ample cause to invade, but not until that threatening storm has actually begun to gather. There is also something quite disingenuous about using Saddam's genocide as a pretext for invasion when the U.S. provided the military means and the political support for it. When Saddam used poison gas against the Kurds in 1988, the Reagan administration not only turned a blind eye to it, but they also prevented the international community from condemning it.[23] To suddenly turn on Saddam for doing what we allowed him to do makes for a contradictory argument. Finally, Hitchens' assertion that Iraq is "shredded" is due in part to the U.S. sponsored sanctions against Iraq, not just Hussein's bellicosity.

The interesting thing about the arguments of both Nichols and Hitchens is that neither author appeals directly to moral principles or to international law, except to point the finger at Iraq. This lacuna allows them to argue in terms of consequential reasoning, appealing to what the future might be if Iraq is not invaded in 2003. This is not a moral appeal but a pragmatic one. As Habermas puts it, pragmatic discourses "serve to relate empirical knowledge to hypothetical goal determinations and preferences and to assess the consequences of (imperfectly informed) choices in the light of underlying maxims." Thus, with pragmatic argumentation, we remain at the level of the factual, empirical, and concrete, and all such claims are chained together, along with the conclusion of a recommended goal or action, through an underlying value commitment, defined as a "preference." This type of discourse, even with goals recommended on the basis of value preferences, remains on the echelon of the empirical. But when we move from the level of pragmatic/consequential discourse to decidedly moral discourse, we move beyond the empirical, concrete claims and engage in "a universal discourse in which all those possibly affected could take part."[24] Another way of stating the concerns of this type of argument is that moral norms become the predominant issue, and "a norm is just only if all can will that it be obeyed by each in comparable situations,"[25] Because utilitarian and pragmatic arguments are not moral ones by this understanding, the issue of humanitarian intervention argued for by Hitchens is moot. Future potential humanitarian crises as *casus belli* are not supported either in ethics, facts, or in international law.

Preventive War Is Not Preemptive. It is important to note from the outset that the invasion of Iraq was to be a first strike, not a response to an attack or an imminent attack by Iraq. That this is so was clearly stated by the Bush administration in their "National Security Strategy of the United States of America," on September 20, 2002. In that publication of official Bush policy, it stated that the U.S. maintains for itself "the option of preemptive actions to counter a sufficient threat to our national security."[26] Although this policy statement uses the term "preemptive," it is more accurate to use the term "preventive." A preventive war is one in which one state wishes to stop another state from acquiring or maintaining the possibility of attacking one's own or another state, prior to that state's actually engaging in the mechanisms for so attacking, such as mobilizing weapons and amassing troops to attack. Such a war would be roundly condemned, both morally and by international law, as we shall see. The definition and ethical considerations for a preemptive war are presented clearly by Michael Walzer. Defining preemptive wars as those of first strike, their moral justification concerns "the point of sufficient threat." A sufficient threat is "a manifest intent to injure, a degree of active preparation that makes that intent a positive danger, and a general situation in which wanting, or doing anything other than fighting, greatly magnifies the risk."[27] As we have already seen, Iraq did not present that kind of threat to the United States prior to March 19, 2003.

To make this more specific, William Galston expands on the criteria Walzer presents and argues that the ethical criteria for preemptive strikes include an analysis of the degree of each of these restraints: 1) the severity of the threat; 2) the degree of probability of the threat; 3) the imminence of the threat; and 4) the cost of delay. When he applies these points of analysis to the situation in Iraq, he finds the following: 1) the threat is high in the worst case—that is, the acquisition of transferable nuclear weapons; 2) the probability of the threat is contested—many experts have argued that a transfer of nuclear weapons by Saddam Hussein to terrorists is contrary not only to his past behavior but also to his clear and present interests; 3) no one has argued that the threat of attack is imminent; 4) the cost of delay is low if it is measured in months as the U.S. tries to exhaust other options.[28]

Since the third and fourth criteria have not been met at all, and the second criterion is disputed, there is no moral case that can be made for a preemptive strike on Iraq.

Finally, it must be recognized on the part of those who trumped up reasons to go to war, that Iraq, no matter what one thinks of its leader, was still a sovereign nation. Any attack on that nation without proper pretext is nothing short of an aggressive action. As Walzer puts it, "[a]ny use of force or imminent threat of force by one state against the political sovereignty or territorial integrity of another constitutes aggression and is a criminal act."[29] The assumption, of course, is that nation-states form a community of sorts, and certain rules of conduct between them are necessary to ensure not only peace, but survival. This is the presumption behind the principle of non-intervention. Walzer thinks that such a principle has for its foundation the rights to life and liberty. This places some very heavy burdens on the nation that wants to enter another with its military for whatever reason: "The burden of proof falls on any political leader who tries to shape the domestic arrangements or alter the conditions of life in a foreign country. And when the attempt is made with armed force, the burden is especially heavy."[30]

Because of the significant requirements for proof of pretext for a preventive war, and because, as we have seen, the proof simply did not exist to take such drastic action, the war against Iraq in 1993 cannot be morally justified. "In the absence of a just cause, there can be no just war."[31]

Proper Intention

Intention deals with the goals of contemplated action. What did the Bush administration intend to be the outcome of the war against Iraq? St. Augustine and the Just War Theory in general refer to the *status quo ante*, such as the restoration of stolen property, territorial integrity, and most of all, peace. Peace must be the ultimate goal of a war. As Augustine states it:

> Peace is the purpose of waging war; and this is true even of men who have a passion for the exercise of military prowess as rulers and commanders.[32]

Again, with St. Thomas Aquinas, the use of the sword is legitimate for those in public authority, where committing violence against an enemy is legitimate if done with the proper inward disposition of charity, where punishment of the enemy is permitted to restore moral order. Where just wars are waged in defense of peace, they are not evil unless the peace they intended is evil.[33]

So what was the intention of the President and his cabinet in going to war?

Was it simply to rid Iraq of Saddam Hussein? That would in no way be permitted by Just War Theory not only because the cause of uprooting a people's leader would not be justified in this case (as we have seen), but because such an action would violate the political sovereignty and territorial integrity of Iraq. The only way to justify the invasion by proper intention is if Saddam had actually done something directly or imminently threatening to the peace and the security of the United States.[34] Short of that, there was no moral reason for military action, and thus no proper intention.

Was it to rid Iraq of WMD's? The U.N. reports completed and released prior to the invasion clearly show that inspections under threat of invasion were working, but they were ignored by the Bush administration. Had their intention been to restore peace or *status quo ante*, they would have adopted the working, ongoing peaceful means of eliminating the weapons they asserted Iraq possessed and/or was pursuing.

Was it to establish democracy in the Mideast? That intention was never stated as the main reason the Bush administration made in its case for invading Iraq. Instead, it came as a *post hoc* reason, after the invasion was already underway. However, this vision is consistent with the neocon position, as we have seen. Nonetheless, as a singular intention for war, it would be immoral, given the requirements of just cause for preventive attacks.

Was it peace? We see no direct statement of this intention in the case for war made by the Bush administration and its supporters. It might be assumed to be the case. Ridding the world of Saddam Hussein and reducing WMD's can only help the cause of peace. There are two things to note here. First, as Augustine states, just cause requires the intention of peace *status quo ante*, not the peace that might someday be disrupted by a menace. Second, if the peace is a *Pax Americana* one, then it is an unstable peace, since someone else's imposed conditions of peace will not be taken lightly by those imposed upon, whether the goal is democracy or not. Those so imposed upon will always seek ways of exploiting the vulnerabilities of the holder of the Pax, when it is from outside of the culture or state. Such is the origin of terrorism, a topic to be dealt with later. So Pax Americana is a temporary and always uncertain peace, not peace in the sense of mutually recognized coexistence between peoples and states.

Exercising the philosophical principle of charity, let us assume that each of the Bush reasons were individually necessary and jointly sufficient conditions of the justification for the invasion. Thus, if there is a possibility that each of the conditions is false, then the case for proper intention fails on logical grounds as well as moral grounds.

Proper Authority

Pro-Invasion Argument

It is interesting that in none of the arguments of the defenders of the invasion of Iraq is there an analysis of who the proper authority is for the U.S. to have legitimate grounds to attack another country. There had been great animus toward the U.N. on the part of the Bush administration and the American people. They had made it clear that they do not need U.N. authorization to pursue preventive war—i.e. wars of U.S. choosing. However, simultaneously and in contradictory fashion, the key players in the Bush administration push to war—Condoleeza Rice, Colin Powell, Dick Cheney, and George Bush—all stated in turn that in attacking Iraq they were enforcing UNSCR 687 and 1441.

In what has to be the most egregious and specious reasoning in support of the Bush administration—but necessary to consider because of their clout in conservative circles--the Heritage Foundation argued that the U.S. does not need to consult the United Nations before it attacks Iraq or any other nation. They base this assertion on four arguments:

Argument One: self-defense. The argument invokes U.N. Charter Article 51, which guarantees the right of every country to self-defense. It rightly applies this to the notion of imminent threat, and then adds that Saddam Hussein is such an imminent threat because "he seeks to develop" WMD.

Analysis: This argument uses "imminent threat," which is defined as an immediately forthcoming military action on the part of another state (i.e. an aggression). There are two ways to understand the term "imminent threat;" one is conceptual, the other is legal. The conceptual definition has been solidified by Michael Walzer in his classic text *Just and Unjust Wars*. Here he makes a distinction between imminent threat and sufficient threat, stating that the legitimacy of a preemptive strike is based not on the former but on the latter. He makes the following claim concerning sufficient threat that has been widely accepted in the literature on war since: "I mean it to cover three things: a manifest intent to injure, a degree of active preparation that makes that intent a positive danger, and a general situation in which waiting, or doing anything other than fighting, greatly magnifies the risk."[35]

In terms of international law, the precedent-setting definition was given by American Secretary of State Daniel Webster, in his rejection of the British explanation for their boarding and attack on the ship *Caroline*. It was quoted by the Nuremberg Tribunal: "preventive action in foreign territory is justified only in case of 'an instant and overwhelming necessity for self-defense, leaving no choice of means, and no moment of deliberation'."[36]

By neither definition was an attack on Iraq justified. Furthermore, the argument that does attempt to justify invasion betrays its weakness when it states that Hussein "seeks" WMD's. That means that he does not possess them, nor is he threatening to use them. Seeking weapons is not the same as an extant threat. Further, even if possession does mean threat, it is only so in the widest possible sense of the word. It certainly does not mean that an attack is sufficient or imminent. Imminence contains within it a notion of immediacy, a definitional criterion not met by Iraq under any such definition. Furthermore, a threat requires an objective act or statement of intention to cause immediate injury to another. Again, Michael Walzer puts it best when he says that a "sufficient threat" requires, among other things, "actual preparation for [a] war [with another nation]."[37] Again, the danger must be immediate for the threat to be imminent or sufficient. This in no way applied to Saddam Hussein in 2003.

Argument Two: the U.S. Constitution. The Heritage argument rests on the claim of authority given to the President "as commander in chief of the armed forces" by the United States Constitution. The argument simply stipulates that "no treaty, including the U.N. Charter, can redistribute this authority."

Analysis: There are at least two problems with this argument. First, the argument does not mention where the Constitution might give the President the power to override other treaties, including something like the U.N. Charter.

This leads to the second point: this argument does not mention Article IV of the Constitution, which, as we have seen, states explicitly that all treaties made by the U.S. become U.S. law. Given this, the only plausible reason the Executive would have to violate his oath to uphold the Constitution (and thus U.S. treaties) would presumably be in the case of self-defense of the the nation. Thus, the Heritage argument from the Constitution is contradictory to their first argument from the U.N. Charter. One cannot appeal to the U.N. Charter and then in the next argument implicitly deny the Charter by quoting the Constitution while at the same time ignoring a part of the Constitution. This contradicts both the first argument, and itself!

Argument Three: existing U.N. Security Council resolution 678, passed in 1990, allowing "member states co-operating with the Government of Kuwait...to use all necessary means" to expel Iraq from occupying Kuwait and to "restore international peace and security in the area." Since this second part has never been completed, the Heritage argument concludes, the U.S. has U.N. authority to enforce this U.N. resolution.

Analysis: First, appeal to a thirteen year-old resolution, even if it "has not been rescinded," is problematic in the sense that it is specific to a time and action taken on the part of Iraq. The resolution never stated that it was intended to be a general mandate of the UNSC. Further, note the specificity of the resolution. It was intended for those states working with Kuwait to expel Iraq; not for Iraq in general. One has to stretch the meaning of the second part of the resolution in order to make the resolution a universal and ongoing mission of the U.N. states. Creating such ongoing goals is something the Charter does, not a particular U.N. resolution.

Finally, notice the contradiction in the Heritage argument. It says that the U.S. has no need of U.N. authorization, then argues that the U.S. is authorized by the U.N. to enforce an old resolution. If the U.S. needs no U.N. authorization, then to use U.N. resolutions to support its authority to act unilaterally is self-defeating, as it tacitly admits U.N. authority for U.S. attacks.

Argument Four: international peace and security. Here the Heritage argument does refer to the Charter, and uses the purpose of the U.N. as stated in Article 1 to permit the U.S. to engage in preventive war with Iraq.

Analysis— If the purpose of the "United *Nations*" is to pursue peace, then it must be through the *united nations* that this is done. It would thus be illegal and improper for one country to engage in establishing a peace of its own definition andmaking.

In general then, the arguments of the Bush administration and of the Heritage Foundation regarding their authority to attack Iraq ignore moral tradition and international law. As we have seen, the arguments favoring an invasion rely heavily on proper authority criteria. "Proper authority," the right of the state to repel its enemies, is sacrosanct, as opposed to individuals or mercenary forces. Repelling the enemy, as Walzer and nearly every other Just War theorist argues, means preemptive, not preventive strikes, are morally legitimate, as has been made clear above.

Second, that the U.S. claimed the authority to invade Iraq on the basis of UNSCR 687 and 1441 indicates that it tacitly recognized the authority of the United Nations to authorize the use of military force. If this is the case, the U.S. does not have the right to enforce a U.N. resolution unilaterally, since the U.N. Charter, Chapter VII, Articles 39 & 40 authorize only the U.N. Security Council to make the determinations regarding who is breaking the peace and what actions should be taken. The only exception to this is in Article 51, which allows a military response to another nation only when one nation is attacked or an attack is imminent. We will examine this in more detail below.

It is important to note that the U.N. resolutions to which the U.S. referred in justifying its planned invasion is in fact out of the bounds of U.S. authority, since the resolutions, along with the U.N. Charter, specifically authorize the U.N. Security Council to determine breaches of obligations.

Refutation of the Arguments Supporting the Invasion

The idea that the U.S. can bypass international bodies and use only its own authority to send its military into another country presumes that unilateralism trumps international law by allowing one nation to determine what is best for both itself and the world and then to act on it, whether or not it is in concert with the rest of the world. Because it excludes dialogue and more importantly the demands of universality of principle required by ethical thinking, it has no place in a moral analysis of war.

Finally, a violation of the U.N. Charter is concomitantly a violation of Article IV of the U.S. Constitution, which says that "all Treaties made . . . under the Authority of the United States, shall be the supreme Law of the Land."[38]

Therefore, the proper authority criterion is not met by the arguments in support of the invasion of Iraq.

Last Resort

Pro Argument. Thomas M. Nichols states the case for invasion under this category quite bluntly: "There is no longer a credible way to envision any peaceful road to Iraqi disarmament." The stated reason is that Saddam has violated his word to open his weapons to U.N. inspectors. When he did begin to follow through on his promise, he reneged, so he will no doubt do it again. As if to make his case clearer, Nichols asserts that because of this lying, "dictators like Saddam forfeit the right to demand further negation and make military action...the only reliable and permanent means of ending their nuclear and other lethal aspirations."[39]

Analysis. The condition of last resort was quite clearly not met by the Bush administration. In the face of U.N. reports clearly stating that although there were many problems, the inspection process was producing results, the U.S. went to war anyway. That action in no way fulfills the condition of last resort. When there is progress over disputed issues, one cannot put an end to dialogue by claiming that no further negotiations are possible. These are contradictory notions. So the statement Nichols makes that Saddam has no right to demand further negotiation is at sharp odds with both ethical prescriptions and with reality. From the start, the Bush position was "no negotiations."[40]

Probability of Success

Prior to the invasion, there were many assertions by the Bush administration that that the invasion would be "a cakewalk" and the Iraqi people would greet the invading U.S. military as "liberators."[41] Even authors like John Langan argued that the U.S. had "technologically sophisticated and physically overwhelming resources" that guaranteed success in the invasion.[42]

Probability of success deals with the projected consequences of military action. There is a close relationship between this criterion and proportionality, since both deal with an attempt to ascertain projected consequences. Probability of success also includes intention, because the "success" must be defined by that which is intended: a return to the *status quo ante*, which ends with agreement to live a peaceful coexistence.

So what are the conceivable projected results from an Iraq invasion? These issues were dealt with quite thoroughly in two studies, both produced in 2002. First, the American Academy of Arts & Sciences Committee on International Security Studies (hereafter abbreviated AAAS) produced a study entitled "War with Iraq: Costs, Consequences, and Alternatives." Second, the Oxford Research Group (hereafter abbreviated ORG) produced a paper called "Iraq: Consequences of a War." Finally, William A. Galston, in "The Perils of Preemptive War," highlighted the various important consequences that might result from an Iraq invasion by the U.S.

The AAAS report presents an impressively detailed and well documented analysis of the conceivable consequences of a U.S. invasion of Iraq, all of which both individually and collectively call into question the probability of a successful outcome. Rather than elaborate on these speculated consequences, a quick listing of them, along with an explanation where needed, will suffice. We will begin with the plausible positive outcomes enumerated by the report:

- Saddam's reign of brutal tyranny will come to an end.
- The Iraqi people will be liberated.
- The spread of democracy in the Mideast will have begun.
- Respect for U.S. military power will be restored.
- Future threats will be reduced as a consequence of potential foes observing U.S. military power and resolve.
- The stability of a democratic Iraq and the end of an evil dictator will show U.S. morality and leadership in the world.

In addition to these possible positive outcomes, the report elaborates on other, gloomier consequences:

- Costs of U.S. involvement in Iraq could mount if the war becomes too bloody or prolonged .
- WMD's could be used, especially probable if Saddam sees that the end is near.
- Iraq could set their own oil fields ablaze, which would result in billions of dollars in economic losses.
- Iraq could disrupt the flow of oil delivery from the Persian Gulf.
- Fighting in Iraq could be urban and guerilla in style, prolonging the war
- Iraq could launch an international campaign of terrorism.
- Saddam could inflame the tensions in Israel, the West Bank, and Gaza. He was already paying the families of Palestinian suicide bombers, had

aligned himself with Palestinian extremists, both politically and economically.
- Iraq could escalate the war by attacking Israel directly.
- Iraq could attack other nations in the region.
- Saddam could preempt the preventive war of the U.S. by attacking ports, sinking tankers, etc.
- The war on terror issued by President Bush would be distracted. It will certainly divert attention and resources away from Afghanistan, where the focus on al Qaeda was and should be.
- It could undermine international cooperation on fighting terrorism. "The global war on terrorism depends on the extensive collaboration among intelligence services, policing agencies, militaries, and so on."[43] With only Britain and Israel in full support of Bush's plans on Iraq, and other nations such as France and Germany fighting against it on the diplomatic front, future cooperation on the war on terror will be minimal and delayed.
- Attacking Iraq in preventive fashion could lead to the loss of "hearts and minds" in the Arab world, which already harbors hatred toward America and which would no doubt see this as yet another insult of American imperialism.
- Invading Iraq could bring a change in world order, from American cooperation with other nations to unilateralism and self-interested actions alone.
- The preventive war could set a precedent for other countries to do the same.
- The war could damage America's reputation in the world.
- It could undermine U.S. relationships with friends and allies.
- It could undermine America's position as a moral leader in the world.
- U.S. relations with the Arab world may be damaged.
- Saddam's absence could reduce or even eliminate the need of other Arab nations to have the U.S. presence in the Mideast for protection, thus complicating the U.S. presence in the region.
- The war could provoke other nations to the conclusion that possession of WMD's is necessary to deter American aggression.
- The war could inflame anti-American sentiment in Pakistan, thus changing the cooperative role the U.S. and Pakistan have had since 9/11.
- Upsurge of Kurdish nationalism could damage U.S.-Turkey relations.
- Any WMD's in Iraq could be sold underground before the U.S. gets control of things in Iraq.
- The U.S. could get bogged down in Baghdad, both economically and militarily. Even Dick Cheney said this in 1991, defending the decision of President George H.W. Bush not to invade Iraq after expelling Saddam from Kuwait.

- U.S. forces in Iraq could be subject to regular attacks.

The Oxford report makes many of the same observations as does the AAAS study. It adds the following possible consequences.

Positive:

- The war could be quick with few U.S. casualties.
- There could be little economic turmoil in post-war Iraq and U.S.
- A stable regime could be installed fairly soon after the U.S. gained control of the country.

Negative:

- Large numbers of civilian casualties are likely, and the number will grow the longer the U.S. occupies Iraq.
- "The fractured make-up of Iraq, with Kurdish, Sunni, Shi'ite, and Christian elements make it unlikely that a stable government would form with ease."
- If WMD's are used by Iraq, the U.S. could respond with a nuclear weapon.
- Increased opposition to U.S. control of the region will almost certainly increase and spread.

It takes only a cursory examination of these conceivable outcomes to say that even a measured utilitarian calculus would weigh the negative outcomes over the positive ones, thus reducing considerably the probability of success.

Analysis—If establishing democracy was part of our true intention for going to war, then the probability of success is even lower. Iraq had never had experience with democracy. Even more to the point, they were used to dictatorship. The chances of imposing a form of democracy alien to both people and leaders, and doing so by violent overthrow, when there was already suspicion in many Arab minds about U.S. intentions, is a recipe for disaster, not success.

Proportionality

The final necessary condition for having a justified movement into war is achieved when a calculation is made that the overall good that will come from the war outweighs the harms that come from it.

This differs from the requirement of proper intention. Proportionality is an attempt to calculate potential consequences that might be empirically projected and measured, whereas proper intention deals with the willed results of a forthcoming action. The distinction between them takes into account the difference between *motive* and *intention*. The motive of an action concerns the goal being sought, whereas the intention refers to the internal disposition of the agent acting: for what reason do they act? It is the belief or set of beliefs that motivate an agent to act in the way they do. That intention is not to be equated with motive is recognized widely, by philosophers such as John Stuart Mill, and Alan Donagan.[44] Donagan states that intention is what an agent deliberately chooses to do from among various alternatives, whereas a motive (what Donagan calls "purpose") "is a state of affairs the coming about of which is the (an) end to which the plan of action is directed."[45]

In this case, most of the pre-war debate collapsed proportionality and probability of success into a single criterion. But if we take the information contained in both the AAAS and the Oxford reports, we can easily fulfill the proportionality requirement by weighing out the conceivable and probable consequences of our actions. It would seem more plausible, on the basis of this analysis, to conclude that the potential consequences of the invasion would have more of a down side than an up side, and at this point, this criterion would argue against the morality of an invasion of Iraq.

Notes

1. Nicholas D. Kristof, "Hitler on the Nile," *New York Times*, February 23, 2003.
2. Michael Walzer, "What a Little War in Iraq Could Do," *New York Times*, March 7, 2003.
3. Jimmy Carter, "Just War—or a Just War?" *New York Times*, March 9, 2003.
4. Langan, John, S.J. "Is There a Cause for War Against Iraq?" November 13, 2002 (unpublished).
5. President Bush made this claim in his State of the Union Address on January 28, 2003 and on March 19, 2003, signaling the start of the invasion. He also made similar claims in speeches on September 12 & 26, 2002; October 7, 2002; February 8, 2003; May 29, 2003. Vice President Cheney made the claim on August 26, 2002; March 24, 2002; March 16, 2003. Each of the speeches referred to in this paragraph may be accessed at www.americanprogress.org.
6. President Bush made this claim in a letter to Congress on March 19, 2003; Vice President Cheney said this on September 14, 2003.
7. Vice President Cheney made this claim on September 14, 2003 and on January 22, 2004; President Bush made it in a speech on September 25, 2002, on September 17, 2003, and in his speech to the U.N. on September 23, 2003.
8. Nichols, Thomas M. "Just War, Not Prevention," *Ethics & International Affairs*, 17.1 (April, 2003).
9. Hitchens, Christopher, "A War to be Proud Of," *The Weekly Standard*, September 5, 2005. While this article was a post-invasion contribution, it summarizes and recapitulates the arguments Hitchens had made prior to the invasion, and this makes it a more convenient source than collating his previous contributions.
10. Blix, Hans, "Notes for Briefing the Security Council," http://www.un.org/Depts/unmovic.
11. El Baradei, "Status of the Agency's Verification Activities in Iraq as of 8 January 2003," http://www.iaea.org/worldatom/Press/Statements/2003.
12. See Cortright, David, Alistair Millar, George A. Lopez, and Linda Gerber, "Contested Case: Do the Facts Justify the Case for War in Iraq?" *A Report of the Sanctions and Security Project of the Fourth Freedom Forum and the Joan B. Kroc Institute for International Peace Studies at the University of Notre Dame*, February 6, 2003.
13. Ibid., p. 7.
14. Ibid., p. 12.
15. See http://www.fair.org/press-releases/kamel.pdf.
16. In the "Preface."
17. For more detail on this, see Immanuel Kant, *Groundwork of the Metaphysic of Morals*, 1785. For a modern interpretation, see John Rawls, *A Theory of Justice* (Cambridge: Harvard University Press, 1971), or *Law of Peoples* (Harvard University Press, 1999). See also the works of Jurgen Habermas, beginning with *Knowledge and Human Interest* (Boston, 1971).
18. *Between Facts and Norms*, pgs. 161—162.
19. See Noam Chomsky, *Failed States*, pgs. 5—6.
20. Ibid, pgs. 85—6.
21. Chomsky, *Hegemony or Survival*, pgs. 9—10.
22. Michael Walzer, *Just and Unjust Wars*, p. 108.

23. See Jon Wiener, "America's Complicity in Saddam's Crimes," *The Nation*, December 30, 2006. See also the Human Rights Watch report on this issue in 1993.
24. Jurgen Habermas, "On the Employments of Practical Reason," *Justification and Application*, pgs. 10—12.
25. Habermas, *Between Facts and Norms*, p. 161.
26. "The National Security Strategy of the United States of America," 2002, http://www.whitehouse.gov/nsc, pg. 15.
27. Walzer, Michael, *Just and Unjust Wars*, pg. 81. It is interesting to note that whereas Walzer defines "preventive war" as one "fought to maintain the balance, to stop what is thought to be an even distribution of power from shifting into a relation of dominance and inferiority," in fact the Bush administration in their "National Security Strategy" of 2002 defines it essentially the opposite way; i.e. to prevent a balance of power between the U.S. and any other country.
28. Galston, William A. "The Perils of Preemptive War," *Philosophy & Public Policy Quarterly*, Vol. 22, n. 4, Fall, 2002, pg. 3.
29. Walzer, op. cit., p. 62.
30. Ibid., p. 86.
31. John Langan, "Is There a Just Cause for War Against Iraq?" *State of the Nation*, Issue 4.1, Winter/Spring, 2003.
32. *City of God*, XIX, 12.
33. See *Summa Contra Gentiles*, III, 140 & 146 for this.
34. The use of the term "directly" threatening refers to the imminence of the threat. As we have seen, there was no imminent threat from Saddam Hussein.
35. Walzer, op. cit., p. 81.
36. The interior quote is from Webster. Quoted in Duncan E.J. Currie, "Preventive War and International Law after Iraq," www.globelaw.com, May 22, 2003.
37. Walzer, op. cit, pg. 81.
38. In full, Article IV says: "This Constitution, and the Law of the United States which shall be made in Pursuance thereof; and all Treaties made, or which shall be made, under the Authority of the United States, shall be the supreme Law of the Land; and the Judges in every State shall be bound thereby, any Thing in the Constitution or Laws of any State to the Contrary notwithstanding."
39. Thomas M. Nichols, "Just War, Not Prevention," *Ethics and International Affairs*, Vol. 17, n. 1, Spring, 2003.
40. Risen, James, "Iraq Said to Have Tried to Reach Last-minute Deal to Avert War," *The New York Times*, November 6, 2003. In November, 2003, the international media discovered that Saddam Hussein had made a last minute effort to avoid the invasion, by expressing his intention to submit to all American demands. That offer was rebuffed by the U.S.
41. "Cakewalk" was the term used by Assistant Defense Secretary Ken Adelman in his op-ed piece arguing in favor of the invasion, in the *Washington Post*, February 13, 2002. The "liberator" comment came from Vice President Cheney, on March 16, 2003, in the NBC program "Meet the Press." For more on this, see http://democrats.senate.gov/dpc.
42. Langan, op. cit.
43. American Academy of Arts & Sciences Committee on International Security Studies, "War with Iraq: Costs, Consequences, and Alternatives," pg. 26.
44. For Mill, see *Utilitarianism*, Ch. 2.

45. Alan Donagan, *The Theory of Morality* (Chicago: The University of Chicago Press, 1977), pgs. 121-131.

Chapter Four
The Ethical Case against the Conduct of the Invasion and Occupation of Iraq

We have seen in detail in the preceding chapters that the U.S. has clearly violated nearly every tenet of moral and legal codes in invading Iraq. If this is clear enough, it is even clearer that the actual conduct of the war, once we commenced with it, was nothing short of a gross violation of the principles of the proper conduct of war—i.e. the ethical parameters, internationally recognized, in fighting a war. These ethical boundaries are contained in the principles of discrimination and proportionality. To this we will add a third section, made necessary by the actions of the U.S. in Afghanistan, Iraq, and elsewhere, such as Guantanamo Bay, Cuba: bans on the use of torture.

Discrimination

Traditionally, the principle of discrimination has been defined in terms of the intention of the agents conducting the war. The operative method used has been the principle of double effect: That is, the intention of the agent must be for the good end (i.e. destruction of the enemy weapons or soldiers at which aim is taken), while the likelihood of the bad end (i.e. killing of civilians) is known but not intended.

But there are problems in using this traditional concept. First of all, it is difficult to see how one can be said not to intend in some way a negative consequence that they know will accompany their action. If intention by necessity be for an end, and if one may properly be said to intend the *good* end, it seems like an artificial and strained justification to say that one does not intend the bad end but simply "foresees" the negative consequences. In other words, double effect simply provides a rationalization for engaging in actions in which the outcome has (at least partly) negative effects. It would be more intellectually honest to state that one intends the act and *all* of the consequences one has determined will result from it, but simply has less of an intention to cause the negative consequences. That is part of the notion of taking responsibility for negative consequences that one is often said not to have "intended;" for example, first and second degree murder. If one absolutely does not intend the negative consequences one foresees, then one is morally bound not engage in the action. The doctor who removes the fallopian tube with the fertilized embryo implanted in it certainly intends to some degree that this fertilized egg will perish. It would take some real rationalization (or at least hair-splitting casuistry) to state: "I know the fertilized egg will perish as the direct result of my action, but I don't really mean for that to happen." It may be a secondary intention, but it is still an intention that the egg perish, and even secondary intentions can be said to be those that deliberately allow something to happen.[1] An advocate of Double Effect might reply that the principle of double effect does distinguish between good intention and intention of negative means. However, the similarities in many instances is so close that it is hard to differentiate them sufficiently to say with any degree of moral confidence that we may say that the means are unintended; as for example, when someone kills an attacker in self-defense and claims not to have intended the death but only the self-defense.[2] Is the death of the attacker even foreseen in such a case? All voluntary actions—i.e. those susceptible to moral analysis—are those done knowingly, and certainly knowledge of negative effects such as someone's death as a result of my shooting them, are encompassed in this conception of voluntary actions. The best way to deal with this problem is to state that the negative effect, while encompassed by what Jeremy Bentham calls "oblique intention,"[3] is nonetheless recognized as such by the agent, who deliberately attempts to minimize the damages she believes must or will occur by the intended act with its (intended) mixed consequences. At this point, however, we would move beyond the traditional notion of the principle of double effect, the examination of which is beyond our purview here. Nevertheless, the notion that intention has degrees leads to the second point of issue with double effect.

How is anyone ever of pure intention, at least pure enough to know that one only intends the good consequences which result from an action? In other words, our intentions are mostly mixed and rarely purified enough to say unequivocally that one intends only a good end. For example, one may desire something and that emotional element may have a strong, yet unconscious effect on one's action. But one cannot say that this desire is part of one's intention. It is unconscious to her or him. This is especially true in times of war. Thus, the principle of double effect has limited use.

Third, double effect can be used as justification for inherently immoral actions. This is not to argue that it is logically committed to doing so, nor that it will inevitably do so. For example, the notion of "collateral damage" is a term that seems to have been sanctioned, if not invented by the use of the principle of double effect: one did not *intend* to kill all those civilians, just the enemy. The civilian casualties were side-effects of the good intention of defeating the enemy. Regardless of the secondary utilitarian calculation of proportionality required by the double effect principle—that the negative not override the positive consequences—there could still be great evil done under the umbrella of double effect if the defeat of the enemy had importance great enough to kill high numbers of civilians.

Fourth, the principle of double effect gives no consideration to what is colloquially called "groupthink" that occurs in organized groups of people, such as an army in battle. One does not consider one's intention at all in such times. In fact, military training precisely takes this dimension of human reason out of the equation. They build in obedience to authority which solidifies the group influence mentality.[4] As social psychologist David G. Myers states it: "Group situations may cause people to lose self-awareness, with resulting loss of individuality and self-restraint."[5] It would be difficult, under such group conditions, to posit an "intention" at all, let alone a rational calculus of double effect.

Finally, when one is forced to act with split-second decision-making, as one does in war, it becomes difficult to know what one's intention really is except "to kill or be killed." Even this is more instinctual than intentional. The necessary discriminations that the principle of double effect requires would be quite difficult to fathom or maintain on the battlefield. There is simply not enough time to deliberate about intention. It is in such moments that character and training, not intention, take over and dominate the actor.

In his book *The Ethics of War*, C.A.J. Coates refutes the criticism that intention has degrees by maintaining that such a notion is incorporated into the principle of double effect.[6] On his reading of the principle (which he denies is a principle, but rather a method of moral analysis), one must intend only the good, and that if one does embrace by intention all consequences, including the evil outcomes, then the act is immoral. That is why, Coates argues, the method of double effect must take into account four elements, not just one. The other three include a pre-moral analysis of the act and its context, the consequences, and proportionality.

But even with the eloquent defense Coates presents, the principle still does not escape the problem of intentional degrees so quickly. First of all, the question still remains as to how it is possible that our intent could be so pure as to not *at all* will any of the evil consequences that are said to be simply foreseen. Second, the defense Coates presents to this criticism clearly shifts the ground of discourse from intention to proportionality. In fact, Coates finishes his embrace of the criticisms of intention in the section on proportionality. So the part of double effect which discusses pure intention is suddenly secondary to the proportion of the good and evil consequences that actually result from the intended act. Finally, there remain the problems already highlighted, such as purity of intention, group-think, etc.

Some of these difficulties are ameliorated by Michael Walzer, who has expanded the traditional concept of double effect to that of "double intention:"

> first, the 'good' be achieved; second, that the foreseeable evil be reduced as far as possible . . . aware of the evil involved, he seeks to minimize it, accepting costs to himself.[7]

By adding this second dimension, Walzer expands the concept of intention, and it allows him to conclude that in the judgment of intention, what "we look for in such cases is some sign of a positive commitment to save civilian lives.... And if saving civilian lives means risking soldier's lives, the risk must be accepted."[8]

Note that Walzer's notion of intention takes it out of the realm of solely subjective states and introduces an element of objectivity by advocating an examination of the results of action as evidence by which to judge intention. Although one may use Walzer's criteria to determine whether individual acts in war are to be morally condemned, the category of discrimination also looks to understand the conduct of the war overall. In this respect, using the criteria of "looking for signs" of intention, the only conceivable measurement of discrimination in the conduct of war would then be an objective one, and that measurement would almost have to be in the form of an inductive argument using the method of proportionality. That is, one or two or three episodes of misconduct in war (i.e. direct and intentional attacks on civilians) are to be condemned in themselves, but they do not usually add up to the conclusion that the war itself is being fought indiscriminately. However, when the individual acts reach a certain unknown and amorphous number in relation to the goal of winning the war, one is on good grounds to question the morality of the war's conduct.

Note, though, that Walzer is careful not to put the matter this way. For him, "due care" trumps proportionality: "they must risk soldiers before they kill civilians," even if the number of civilians to be killed collaterally is small.[9] It remains an open question how one is to make this assessment of the overall conduct of the war.

So it would seem that *jus in bello* judgment relies in the first instance on discrimination and only secondarily on proportionality, since proportionality serves the interest of "looking for signs" of saving civilian lives. Thus, discrimination is the prior moral category for *jus in bello* evaluation. Whenever civilians are indiscriminately killed, the war is being fought immorally, regardless of proportionality. The problem is that a few such incidences do not make for the overall immoral conduct of a war. When the practice of either ignoring (i.e. not taking into account) or intending civilian deaths becomes commonplace, whether proportional or not to the good intention of defeating the enemy, the war itself may be said to be conducted unjustly. When it is part of the command structure, the injustice of the fighting is a *fait accompli*. That is to say, proportional or not, if indiscriminate killing becomes a significant feature of the means of fighting the war, no end can justify it. Hence the priority of discrimination to proportionality is argued for on the grounds of the special or higher value we place on civilian lives over military objectives. Although in judging war's conduct, the *numbers* of civilians killed certainly matters and is certainly a *lack* of "a sign of a positive commitment to save civilians lives," it is not the only, nor is it the decisive criterion for determining the overall conduct of the war. How the civilians came to be killed is decisive, because it tells us directly about the conduct of the war. In the case of Iraq, what is required for discrimination in this sense is to collate the myriad reports of U.S. soldier targeting of and abuse of civilians in Iraq (and elsewhere if the category is the so-called "war on terror").

Let us begin with this assertion: the Bush administration and its generals have not considered the category of discrimination to be of importance. This is directly reflected in at least two events: the admission of the U.S. military that it no longer counts the civilian dead in Iraq, and the order that was issued in December of 2003 from the newly formed Iraqi government, with support from the (U.S.) Coalition Provisional Authority, to stop counting the Iraqi dead civilians.[10] If it was truly U.S. policy to protect noncombatants and to avoid injuring or killing them, one would think that knowing how many they have killed or for whose deaths they are at least partly responsible would be something the military would want to know and engage, not suppress.

In conjunction with this, a controversial report concerning the deaths of Iraqi civilians was issued by the prestigious medical journal, *The Lancet*. In the October 12, 2006 issue, it reported that, by the end of 2005, 600,000 Iraqis had died violently due to the war. While this does not imply that all of these deaths were due directly to U.S. troops and bombings, a significant number of them would have to be so attributed, as we shall see below. Further, these civilian casualties are the direct result of the U.S. invasion, so the U.S. bears responsibility for them. While the Bush administration rejects the method by which this number was arrived, it is important to recognize that the U.S. government had used the same method and some of the same researchers for tabulating the same numbers in Darfur, Kosovo, and after Katrina in New Orleans.[11] This report was corroborated by a Johns Hopkins report also released in October of 2006, claiming that 654,000 Iraqi deaths were caused by the U.S. invasion. In this report, gunshots were said to be the leading cause of death, at 56%. Airstrikes and bombs accounted for 13-14% of the civilian fatalities.[12]

We must add two massacres to this ever-growing category of civilian abuse inflicted by the U.S. incursion into Iraq: Haditha and Fallujah. On November 19, 2005, near the western Iraqi town of Haditha, a roadside bomb struck a U.S. Marine humvee, killing one of the Marines inside. In retaliation, the Marines went on a rampage in Hadith, massacring 24 civilians while they slept. The Marines originally denied the story, and said that gunmen from the city opened fire on them, and that 24 were killed in the exchange. However, the testimony of eyewitnesses and the aftermath filmed by a videographer soon told the world the true story: the civilians were still in their beds in their nightclothes, and the insides of their houses were pockmarked with bullet holes. Seven women and five children were among the dead.[13] Now eight Marines have been charged in the killing of the 24 civilians.[14]

In November of 2004, the U.S. military engaged in an assault on the city of Fallujah that made the original start of the war pale in comparison. Perhaps the most succinct formulation of the events there was described by Marjorie Cohn, professor at Thomas Jefferson School of Law, executive vice president of the National Lawyers Guild, and the U.S. representative to the executive committee of the American Association of Jurists:

Between 10,000 and 15,000 U.S. troops with warplanes and artillery have begun to invade the Iraqi city of Fallujah. To 'soften up' the rebels, American forces dropped five 500-pound bombs on 'insurgent targets.' The Americans destroyed the Nazzal Emergency Hospital in the center of town. They stormed and occupied the Fallujah General Hospital, and have not agreed to allow doctors and ambulances go inside the main part of the city to help the wounded.[15]

Associated Press journalist Helen Thomas gives a similar account of this assault, adding that 900 civilians were killed as a direct result of the U.S. military attack.[16] Rory McCarthy from *The Guardian U.K.* added that Iraqi Red Crescent and other aid vehicles were denied entry into Fallujah by the U.S. military for days after the attack.[17]

One year later, Italian television documented a story showing that the United States used both cluster bombs and white phosphorus bombs on the citizens of Fallujah.[18] White phosphorus works in a similar fashion to napalm, in that it burns whatever it touches. It can burn through clothes and even gas masks, and burns the victim to death. That could be one reason the injury count from Fallujah was so low at 1,000, while the death rate was so high. One way or another, the use of such bombs is strictly prohibited not only by the ethical principle of discrimination, but by international law. White phosphorus does not discriminate who it kills, and when used on a population—even if one intends only to kill the guerrillas among them—it kills everyone in its path. These actions, as well as the assault on Fallujah in general, violate the Geneva Convention and the War Crimes Act of 1996. As for the violation of the ethical principle of discrimination, Michael Walzer has said it best: if there is no distinction possible between the guerrillas and the civilians,

> the anti-guerrilla war can then no longer be fought—and not just because, from a strategic point of view, it can no longer be won. It cannot be fought because it is no longer an anti-guerrilla but an anti-social war, a war against an entire people.[19]

Haditha and Fallujah were both war crimes that the U.S. military attempted to cover up. But according to press reports, there are many more such incidents that occur in Iraq that never get reported, such as the civilian massacres in Balad, al-Latifya, Samara, Najaf, and others.[20] In Najaf alone over 200 civilians were massacred by U.S. forces.[21] Perhaps the most telling report, however, comes from a detailed study done by *The Nation* magazine. Released June 30, 2007, the magazine interviewed fifty veterans of the Iraq war, and documented their stories in detail. The soldiers not only confirmed stories like the ones in Haditha and Fallujah, but told their own stories of their attacks on civilians. It makes for disturbing reading.[22]

Here are two other stories among the all-too-many that could have been listed here concerning the way the U.S. military is conducting the war. First, the Pentagon acknowledged that it was about to put kidnapping teams into Iraq to "advise, support and possibly train" Iraqi death squads to track down and kidnap or kill suspected terrorist leaders.[23] Second, the U.S. admitted to its preparation to use CS gas, pepper spray, and "calmative" gasses similar to the one that killed 120 hostages in Moscow in 2002 on Iraqis, in direct violation of the Chemical Weapons Convention.[24]

There have been numerous reports about the U.S. military arresting reporters in Iraq, and torture them while detaining them. This has happened to reporters from Reuters, CBS, the Italian News Service, al-Jazeera, Al-Arabiya, the Spanish Network, and French-Canal.[25] The most famous instances occurred in the arrest and detention of reporters in Fallujah (Reuters and Al-Arabiya), the U.S. bombing of al-Jazeera's Baghdad office, and the U.S. tank firing on the Palestinian Hotel, the headquarters of foreign journalists. In the latter two episodes, three journalists were killed.

United States occupation forces have also been storming and bombing hospitals in Iraq, although there are mixed stories regarding these incidents. In some cases, it appears that sniper gunfire was directed at U.S. soldiers from a hospital roof. By international law, should that happen, that hospital would lose its immunity from attack. However, this is not the case in all U.S. attacks. For example, in Ramadi, Najaf, Fallujah, Mosul, and Anbar, U.S. forces have raided and occupied the hospitals there, sometimes interfering with doctors and health care professionals by repeatedly handcuffing them, and sometimes preventing the wounded from getting to the hospital by ambulance. The fact that the Mahdi army, the followers of Moqtada al-Sadr, and other insurgent armies do the same thing, does not justify similar U.S. actions.[26]

According to Colonel Dan Smith, there are a growing number of abuse cases of U.S. soldiers of civilians in Iraq, among them:

- A Marine squad accused of killing 24 civilians and members of the chain-of-command falsifying or failing to investigate the incident (Haditha);
- Five soldiers accused of premeditated rape of an Iraqi teenager and murdering her and her family (Mahmoudiya);
- Marines accused of killing an Iraqi civilian and then planting an AK-47 beside his body (Ramadi);
- Marines accused of assaulting detainees during interrogation;
- Preliminary enquiries into an alleged order from an Army brigade commander to "kill all military aged males" and the subsequent deaths of there Iraqi men (Salahuddin).[27]

Although there are literally hundreds of stories that were collected for this section, these should be sufficient to make it obvious that the war in Iraq is being conducted in a gruesome, horrific, and bloody manner against the civilians of Iraq (and elsewhere). We are brutalizing the people of Iraq. According to an ACLU study, released in January of 2005, there is widespread physical abuse of Iraqi civilians by the U.S. military, including electric shocks, forced sodomy, cigarette burns, aggressive dogs, sexual humiliation, beatings, and waterboarding.[28] An independent study by the Pentagon confirmed the ACLU accusations.[29] As many as 90 incidents took place at Adhamiya Palace, one of the residences of Saddam Hussein, in eastern Baghdad. Thus, the well-known torture cases from Abu Ghraib prison are not isolated. All of these come under the category of torture, which we must discuss.

Proportionality

The means used to win the war cannot overshadow the end of victory. The use of torture and also targeting and indiscriminately harming and killing civilians in the numbers we have cannot in any way meet this requirement of proportionality. Proportionality requires that the good that results must outweigh the evils of the war. The damage that has been done to Iraq is inestimable, but estimate it we must if we are to judge the conduct of the war from a moral perspective. Certainly some of the more dire possible consequences listed by the Academy of Arts & Sciences Committee on International Security Studies and also the Oxford group have come to pass:

- Costs of U.S. involvement in Iraq are mounting by the day, and the war has becomes bloody and prolonged.
- Fighting in Iraq has become urban and guerilla in style, prolonging the war.
- The war on terror issued by President Bush has diverted attention and resources away from Afghanistan, where the focus on al Qaeda was and should be.
- We have yet to see if the war has undermined international cooperation on fighting terrorism. We have also yet to see if attacking Iraq in preventive fashion has also led to the loss of "hearts and minds" in the Arab world. Neither of these negative consequences can be ruled out at this time, however.
- The war could damage America's reputation in the world, and has undermined America's position as a moral leader in the world.
- The war has inflamed anti-American sentiment in Pakistan.
- The U.S. has become bogged down in Baghdad, both economically and militarily.
- U.S. forces in Iraq have been subject to regular attacks.
- Large numbers of civilian casualties are occurring, and the number will grow the longer the U.S. occupies Iraq.
- The fractured make-up of Iraq, with Kurdish, Sunni, Shi'ite, and Christian elements has not only hampered the formation of a stable government in Iraq, but has led to civil war.
- Perhaps most significantly, terrorist organizations have increased their numbers significantly since the invasion. The National Intelligence Estimate, declassified by the U.S. in September of 2006, stated that "the Iraq conflict has become the 'cause célèbre' for jihadists, breeding a deep resentment of U.S. involvement in the Muslim world and cultivat-

ing supporters for the global jihadist movement." The report represented a consensus of 16 U.S. spy agencies.[30]

It would appear that, four years into the invasion, these negative consequences have outweighed the good that has been done by the elimination of Saddam Hussein. Since no WMD's were found, and since it has come to light that the use of intelligence information on the part of the Bush administration was skewed to their pre-formed ideology regarding the Mideast and America's role there, an Iraq without its WMD's cannot be labeled as a good consequence of the invasion.

Thus, while there is still the possibility that the U.S. will pull this war out of the flames of injustice and salvage it into an overall good, it does not look that way at this time. The requirement of proportionality has not met in the conduct of this war.

Torture

The use of torture by the military against citizens of any country, suspects or not, is a sure sign of a country that has lost its moral way. That the U.S. tortures will be the first part of the analysis to come; that it is manifestly immoral and illegal will comprise the second part of the analysis. Although the latter part should be obvious to those with a conscience or who know the principles of morality behind the letter of international law, it is not obvious to the Bush administration, the military generals who order and participate in it, and to the soldiers who engage in it.

A fifty-three page report written on torture at Abu Ghraib by Major General Antonio M. Taguba is well-enough known by now to allow us to dispense with all but a brief summary of the details of the widespread "sadistic, blatant, and wanton criminal abuses" that occurred there. Although the sources of the immediate abuse were the 372nd Military Police Company, the 800th MP Company, and the 320th MP Company, Taguba also named the American intelligence community as being deeply involved in torture and civilian abuse.

According to Taguba, the abuse of suspected citizens at Abu Ghraib included

> Breaking chemical lights and pouring the phosphoric liquid on detainees; pouring cold water on naked detainees; beating detainees with a broom handle and a chair; threatening male detainees with rape; allowing a military police guard to stitch the wound of a detainee who was injured after being slammed against the wall in his cell; sodomizing a detainee with a chemical light and perhaps a broom stick, and using military working dogs to frighten and intimidate detainees with threats of attack, and in one instance actually biting a detainee.[31]

In fact, the abuse reported at Abu Ghraib is the same as that in Afghanistan and Guantanamo Bay prison in Cuba. All three places—and numerous other "black hole" sites, where U.S. prisoners have "disappeared"[32]—have shown a regular and repeated pattern of physical and psychological torture:

> hooding, loud noises, the 'stress positions,' the sexual humiliations, the threatened assaults, and the forced violations—all seem to emerge from the same script, a script so widely known that apparently even random soldiers the Reuters staffers encountered in moving about the Volturno base knew their parts and were able to play them. All of this...suggests a clear program that had been purposely devised and methodically distributed with the intention, in the words of General Sanchez's October 12 memorandum, of helping American troops 'manipulate an internee's emotions and weaknesses'.[33]

Mark Danner presented a remarkable examination of the patterns of torture he had unearthed from various U.S. military sites in Afghanistan, Guantanamo Bay, and Iraq. He concluded with this assessment: "Different soldiers, different unit, different base; and yet it is obvious that much of what might be called the 'thematic content' of the abuse is very similar."[34] Brian Whitaker of *The Guardian* newspaper of London acknowledged the same, stating further that "the U.S. holds detainees at Bagram, Kandahar, Jalalabad and Asadabad, where there have been complaints of being severely beaten, doused with cold water, [and] forced to stay awake or made to stand or kneel in painful positions for long periods."[35] This was confirmed by two British journalists who were arrested by U.S. soldiers and held at Guantanamo Bay. They were arrested in Afghanistan, imprisoned there, and then moved to Guantanamo, where they were kept without charge for two years, then released. They described the same patterns of torture in both places: "assaults on prisoners, prolonged shackling in uncomfortable positions, strobe lights, loud music and being threatened with dogs."[36]

All of this was sanctioned by higher-ups in the Bush White House, such as Attorney General Alberto Gonzalez and Defense Secretary Donald Rumsfeld. Gonzalez, for his part, wrote a memo in January of 2002 that stated that "The war against terror is a new kind of war . . . this new paradigm renders obsolete Geneva's strict limitations on questioning of enemy prisoners and renders quaint some of its provisions." "Gonzalez also designed the military commissions to deny due process to those who will face trials in them."[37] This was further supported and developed by a memo written in 2004 which defined torture so narrowly that "the torturer would have to nearly kill the torturee in order to run afoul of the legal prohibition against torture."[38] Rumsfeld himself was said to have "micromanaged torture." He was the first to refer to the detainees at Guananamo as "unlawful combatants" who "do not have any rights under the Geneva Conventions." He personally decided whether interrogators could use stress positions; he authorized "taking the gloves off" for interrogators questioning John Walker Lindh, an American citizen who became a member of the Taliban, and was captured in Afghanistan. In a sworn 55-page statement by Air Force Lt. General Randall Schmidt, appointed to investigate FBI charges that there was widespread abuse going on at Guantanamo, Schmidt stated that Rumsfeld was personally involved in the general stresses put upon prisoners."[39]

The reaction from the U.S. government to these allegations has been predictable: denial, delays on investigations, rationalizations, and secrecy. However, as if to admit their guilt, the White House sought, and received, exception from the abuse ban, in the Military Commissions Act of 2006.[40]

Analysis

Contrary to the statements of the U.S. Attorney General, the internationally accepted definition of torture comes from the *U.N. Convention against Torture* (UNCAT, which came into force in June, 1987): "the intentional infliction of severe physical or mental pain or suffering for purposes such as obtaining information or a confession, or punishing, intimidating or coercing someone." Treating civilians in such fashion would be illegal, according to this convention.

The ethical principles concerning torture are mainly Kantian, and universally considered to be an extreme violation of human rights. The reason for this is that any conduct toward another that is a physical or psychological attack on the humanness/human dignity of another—i.e. is degrading or dehumanizing—is inherently immoral. It does not treat humanity as an end, but rather as a means.

Torture, from this point of view, would be immoral because of the attempt to control another person's body and mind by eliciting responses to intended painful stimuli. As such, it destroys the rights of persons to physical and psychological integrity (i.e. independence) rather than limiting it. Further, we may make the following brief moral observations regarding torture. It is the recognition of the moral weight of these observations that has produced both domestic and international law proscribing torture.

- allowing torture removes all moral boundaries regarding what one human may do to another, or what one government may do to another human.
- Fundamental rights to be treated humanely are inalienable, regardless of a person's conduct.
- Torture is a direct contradiction to democracy, which is predicated on the notion that people have rights. *All* rights are taken away in torture practices.
- Every moral code begins with the notion "do no harm." Whether theistic or atheistic, deliberately inflicting pain on another human for whatever ends has always been morally anathema.

There are also cogent utilitarian arguments against torture. For example, psychological torture has been shown to cause mental harm which can persist for years after it was administered. Those who have been tortured with "stress and duress" torture (e.g. sleep deprivation, prolonged isolation, fake drowning, nakedness and sexual humiliation, sensory deprivation, stress positions) call it "never ending." The reasons: sleep deprivation leads to cognitive impairment, including attention deficits and impaired memory, reasoning, verbal communication, and decision-making. Prolonged isolation results in inability to concentrate, disorientation, hallucinations, and depression.[41]

There are also moral questions that are difficult to answer once torture is permitted. For example, once torture commences, it is impossible to identify a clear stopping point. At what point do we stop causing a person pain if he refuses to talk after pain application methods? What do we do if the information gained under torture is a lie, spoken to stop the pain from being administered to him or her? Further, there is no known state that tortures "only a little." In fact, every study shows that states that use torture and ill-treatment use it broadly and supplement it with other repressive measures.[42] Finally, if the end justifies the means, does that not permit terrorists to argue in the same fashion?

The pragmatic form of argument would add to this that torture fails more often than it works, since those interrogated by such techniques frequently provide information they believe their interrogators want, just to stop the pain. For example, Lieutenant Harry E. Soyster, former chair of the Defense Intelligence Agency, made the following statement regarding torture:

> The reality is that use of torture produces inconsistent results that are an unreliable basis for action and policy. The overwhelming consensus of intelligence professionals is that torture produces unreliable information.[43]

That torture is heartily disapproved of by nations worldwide, we may demonstrate by enumerating some international laws concerning torture:

A. *U.N. Convention against Torture*: Articles 1, 2, 3, and 16

Article 1, Section 1: Torture is defined as "any act by which severe pain or suffering, whether physical or mental, is intentionally inflicted on a person for such purposes as obtaining from him or a third person information or a confession, punishing him for an act he or a third person has committed or is suspected of having committed, or intimidating or coercing him or a third person, or for any reason based on discrimination of any kind, when such pain or suffering is inflicted by or at the instigation of or with the consent or acquiescence of a public official or other person acting in an official capacity."

Section 2: If a nation has signed the treaty without reservations, then there are *no exceptional circumstances whatsoever* where a nation can use torture.

Article 2, Section 1: Each State Party shall take effective legislative, administrative, judicial or other measures to prevent acts of torture in any territory under its jurisdiction.

Section 2: No exceptional circumstances whatsoever, whether a state of war or a threat of war, internal political in stability or any other public emergency, may be invoked as a justification of torture.

Section 3: An order from a superior officer or a public authority may not be invoked as a justification of torture.

Article 3: "No State Party shall expel, return or extradite a person to another state where there are substantial grounds for believing that he would be in danger of being subjected to torture."

B. *U.N. Universal Declaration of Human Rights*, Article 5: "No one shall be subjected to torture or to cruel, inhuman or degrading treatment or punishment."

C. Rome Statute of the International Criminal Court
   Article 7: Torture is in the "crimes against humanity"
   Article 8: Torture is a war crime.
D. Geneva Conventions (Third and Fourth)
E. Geneva Conventions Additional Protocols (I & II)
F. European Convention on Human Rights
   Article 3: "Prohibition of torture:" "No one shall be subjected to torture or to inhuman or degrading treatment or punishment."

The United States has signed the Universal Declaration of Human Rights, Geneva Conventions, and UNCAT, but we still torture, and have done so for 50 years.[44] According to Alfred W. McCoy, professor of history at the University of Wisconsin-Madison, the following facts apply to the U.S. government and torture:

1. From 1950-1962, the CIA conducted massive, secret research into coercion and the malleability of human consciousness which, by the late 1950's, was costing a billion dollars a year. This research produced a new method of torture, "no-touch" torture.

2. By 1967, the CIA was operating 40 interrogation centers in South Vietnam that killed over 20,000 Viet Cong suspects.

3. This practice was the same one used in Kabul on Al Qaeda suspects in 2002, and seen in Abu Ghraib.

4. Torture comes with limited utility and a high political price. It is of limited utility because tortured people will say anything to stop the pain. The high political price comes from the fact that at least twice during the Cold War, the CIA's torture training contributed to the destabilization of two key American allies: Iran's Shah and the Philippines' Ferdinand Marcos.

5. U.S. examples of torture parallel the torture done by England in Northern Ireland in the 1970's: 1) minimizing the torture with euphemisms such as "interrogation in depth;" 2) justifying it on grounds that it was necessary or effective; 3) attempting to bury the issue by blaming "a few bad apples."

Unfortunately, there are some lawyers and intellectuals who argue in favor of torture: David Yerushalmi, Alan M. Dershowitz, Michael Ignatieff, and Mirko Bagaric, to name a few. We will take two of these writers as representative of the attempts in the U.S. dialogue to morally and legally permit torture of civilians as happened in Abu Ghraib and still happens in Iraq, Afghanistan, and Guantanamo Bay today. It is interesting to note that every one of these writers argues in strictly utilitarian/pragmatic fashion.[45]

David Yerushalmi, an attorney who sits on the board of trustees of the Institute for Advanced Strategic and Political Studies, a conservative "think tank," couches his argument in terms of "national survival." Specifically, he argues in the form of what he considers to be an exclusive disjunction: either we allow ourselves to torture suspected terrorists or our nation will not survive.[46]

But surely this is a canard. First, a handful of terrorists are unlikely to bring a superpower to its knees. If national survival really was at stake, it would constitute what theorists such as Michael Walzer call "supreme emergency," which allows a nation's survival to override ethical proscriptions and the war conventions. However, the idea of torturing suspected terrorists does not fit the definition of a supreme emergency. Again we resort to Walzer and his definition of "supreme emergency:"

> It is defined by two criteria, which correspond to the two levels on which the concept of necessity works: the first has to do with the imminence of the danger and the second with its nature. The two criteria must both be applied.[47]

As an example of imminence, Walzer presents the Nazi regime and its military conquest of Europe as one "that would surely constitute a supreme emergency."[48] Neither Al Qaeda nor any other terrorist group is anywhere near this level of ability (of invading and conquering the U.S.) so as to constitute the required "imminence" that allows us to override ethical constraints on torturing others, since it is extremely unlikely that the very existence of the state is threatened, even in the face of a concerted and serial planned attack. Even then, this serial and massive attack would have to be nuclear or chemical in its means. This is a "doomsday scenario" that defenders of torture rely upon to attempt to reject contemporary universal bans on it. As such, it is unrealistic, highly improbable, and thus a highly implausible scenario.

Regarding Walzer's second point, the nature of a supreme emergency is such that "the danger must be of an unusual and horrifying kind." Although such a criterion can be put to obvious propagandistic use, Walzer specifies that what he has in mind is something along the lines of the horrible evil of a Nazi takeover of a European nation. That bin Laden is not the moral equivalent of Hitler almost goes without saying. But if one needs proof of this statement, one need only consult the fatwa issued by bin Laden to see this. In it, he is very specific regarding his goals, and they are not evil. He simply wants the U.S. repelled from the holy land of Saudi Arabia, and the Mid East in general. In addition, one must remember that bin Laden does not speak for the Arab world in general, let alone all Muslims, most of whom reject his position. All of this must be pointed out in order to demonstrate the extreme nature of Yerushalmi's and other defenders arguments.

Next, Yerushalmi, in crafting his disjunction between the necessity of torture and national existence, overlooks a simple third disjunct that makes his argument invalid: a nation such as the U.S. might support engaging in a distinctly moral action, such as withdrawing the U.S. military from Saudi Arabia and Iraq. This would significantly lessen the impulse to terrorism against the United States, and thereby disengage any alleged supreme emergency that might permit torture. Yerushalmi implicitly admits that torture is moral only under conditions of supreme emergency. Because of the extreme nature of torture, if there is a less extreme way to reduce an alleged state of supreme emergency, then that is the correct moral route to take.

In conjunction with this false, because exclusive, disjunction, he implies quite strongly that terrorists are "insane" because they "pose a danger to...good men." We can respond both to this notion of the insanity of the terrorist as well as to support the addition of the third disjunct to his argument simply by appealing to the numerous psychological studies of this issue. The psychological literature is filled with information describing terrorism not as a consequence of the insanity of the perpetrators, but as a response to perceived hostile aggression.[49] For one example, Robert A. Pape has compiled a database of every suicide bombing attack around the world from 1980 to 2001. His conclusion is that:

> there is little connection between suicide terrorism and Islamic fundamentalism, or any other religion, for that matter. . . . Rather, what nearly all suicide terrorist campaigns have in common is a specific secular and strategic goal: to compel liberal democracies to withdraw military forces from territory that the terrorists consider to be their homeland.[50]

Pape maintains that the data shows that nearly every suicide bombing is done as part of organized campaigns, not as isolated or random incidents. Further, liberal democracies that are involved in some form of occupation are the targets of almost every suicide attack. While such democracies usually respond with heavy military force, it never works:

> The close association between foreign military occupations and the growth of suicide terrorist movements shows the folly of any strategy centering on conquering countries that sponsor terrorism or in trying to transform their political system.

Thus, the issue is not as simple as "permitting torture or dying as a nation," and a condemnation of torture could well be maintained along with national survival, especially if we add the premise that part of the issue is whether we as a nation are willing to dialogue and compromise with others and to examine the possibility that some of our national military actions are morally wrong and thus require correction.

Yerushalmi goes on to state that the laws on torture suffer from at least two significant problems. First, they are vague and thus inapplicable. Second, law does not deal with whether we "ought" to torture. It only says we are not to do it. So he attempts to craft a moral argument permitting torture on the grounds that it is the "decent" thing to do, by using the Golden Rule. Regarding the first issue, the logic of his argument is faulty: the fact that laws are vague does not imply the conclusion that they are inapplicable. Laws are quite frequently vague and even ambiguous; that is the reason the judicial system has judges, whose job it is to interpret the laws and decide (i.e. judge) where they are applicable and where not. One cannot help but think that perhaps Yerushalmi wants to avoid reference to the law because the law is universal in condemning torture.

Further, as a lawyer, his philosophy of jurisprudence should be more evolved than it is. Rather than playing off of law's inherent ambiguity and vagueness, would it not be more realistic—and more intellectually honest—to acknowledge that one of the reasons for the semantic ambiguity in laws is that laws are in part an expression of moral principles? As Oxford philosophy of law professor Ronald Dworkin puts it:

> Words like 'reasonable,' 'negligent,' 'unjust,' and 'significant,' often perform just this function[:] each of these words makes the application of the rule which contains it depend to some extent upon the principles or policies lying beyond the rule. . . . If we are bound by a rule that says that 'unreasonable' contracts are void, or that grossly 'unfair' contracts will not be enforced, much more judgment is required than if the quoted terms were omitted.[51]

We can take it that, in the case of torture, the universal ban on torture demonstrates not only a solid legal rule, but also significant and deeply held principles concerning respect for human nature that exist as moral underpinnings to the ban. Additionally, such principles demonstrate that there is widespread recognition that the ban on torture is an expression of who we are as human beings (not only as citizens of a state, as Yerushalmi argues), and that the slippery slope of torture and complete disrespect for humans is very easily engaged when allowing some acts of torture. Ambiguous or not, the values of the world community do not permit it.

Regarding the second issue (the "ought" of torture; i.e. the moral argument), Yerushalmi appeals to the Golden Rule, concluding that "a universal Golden Rule not only allows for torture, it demands it in certain circumstances." How does he arrive at such a bizarre conclusion from a command concerning our duties toward others? Let us see.

His example of using the Golden Rule to allow for torture is this:

> [I]f I thought I might have information in the future about bad acts my co-conspirators were going to carry out in an effort to hurt the good men, I would want to make every effort now during my sane moments

to instruct my fellow good men to torture me if necessary in order to protect and to save the innocent and good lives.

With this reworking of the Golden Rule, Yerushalmi twists it out of its ethical meaning. First of all, from the imperative form of informing me how I should act toward others ("Do unto others"), it becomes completely reversed in Yerushalmi's argument: "what I would want *others* to do *to me* if I was sane." The priority shifts from my duties toward others, to their duties toward me. These are two different things, and the Golden Rule is incorrectly cited using his conception of it. The point of the Golden Rule is to present us with a method by which to measure our obligations and conduct toward others, not to determine their conduct toward us. Second, Yerushalmi's Golden Rule shifts it from an imperative form ("Do unto others") to a hypothetical form ("If I was sane"). This shift of form is concomitantly a shift in moral weight, from "all others" to "others in a certain situation." Third, Yerushalmi's version of the Golden Rule shifts from a practical measure of conduct to a hypothetical example of potential conduct. Yerushalmi thus changes its meaning from an ethical command to an ethical hypothesis, and in doing so he goes beyond the clear meaning of the Rule itself.

Third, the Golden Rule in no way allows one to *hurt* others simply because one can hypothesize that one might want to be tortured. It would be entirely masochistic and thus truly "insane" to interpret the Rule as saying "Administer unto others the hurt that you would want them to administer unto you." This leads to the next issue, and that is that Yerushalmi reduces the Golden Rule to an *implausible* hypothetical. Would I want others to torture me if I was sane? It is hardly likely, his assertions to the contrary notwithstanding. Reversibility is what the Golden Rule is about, and Yerushalmi admits that. But reversibility is concerned with how I treat others by putting myself in their shoes, not about how I might want them to treat me if they were in my shoes as I wear them at present. So how can he argue that I would ever want to be tortured? He has smuggled into the Golden Rule a conception of the common good, or better, of numbers of people balanced against me as an individual would-be terrorist: "I would even instruct other good men to kill me if that would, because of my bad behavior, save the lives of other good people." So for Yersushalmi's hypothetical Golden Rule, the common good is what "do unto others" really means—i.e. "Do what is best for the majority." However, that maxim is not contained in the Rule, and by adding it, he commits the logical fallacy of begging the question. That is, he smuggles into the premise of the Golden Rule his notion of the common good, then concludes that for the common good, torture is permitted.

Moreover, there is no moral "ought" to abuse of another human being that may be justified by using the Golden Rule in its intended imperative form ("Do unto others"). The question answered by the Golden Rule is how I must conduct myself toward others, not when I may abuse others.

Nor is there a permissibility clause in the ban on torture in international law. And with good reason, too. Once torture becomes an "ought," any other "ought" is permitted, since torture is the most brutal and abusive action one human can take toward another. There is no Categorical Imperative that would permit it. Second, the law is based on a moral "ought" or "ought not," so indirectly the law does deal with the "ought" issue in that normative concerns underpin law, and it does not permit an "ought" to torture.[52]

It is interesting to note that Yerushalmi follows the standard line of supporters of torture, from the White House on down, and that is to redefine it quite narrowly to include only, as Yerushalmi puts it, "a level of pain that has a reasonable likelihood to cause a normal person under the objective conditions of captivity to suffer permanent physical or non-physical [i.e. psychological] harm." If torture is only about administering permanent harm, then virtually anything goes in interrogation, provided it does not break bones or cause "organ failure, impairment of bodily function, or even death," to use the words of former Bush administration Assistant Attorney General Bybee and presidential counsel David Addington.[53] But when one acknowledges the principle of human respect—or negatively, the condemnation of actions that abuse the person's body or mind—that is behind the laws prohibiting torture, then one can no longer use such extremely narrow definitions. They are at direct odds with the principle that is the lifeblood of the laws banning torture.

But perhaps of all the problems with Yerushalmi's argument, the greatest one is in the assertion he makes that those who say that torture does not elicit the information wanted from the one being tortured—i.e. that torture does not work—are lying. Such people "know it is a bald-faced lie. It can be nothing else." For his support to this very strong allegation, he presents two cases in which he states torture did result in obtaining the wanted information: the cases of Senator John McCain while he was a POW in Vietnam, and the case of Lt. Col. Allen West. In the first case, McCain allegedly admits in his autobiography that he gave up some information under torture that he would not have under other conditions. In the second case, Lt. Col. West, by pointing his pistol at "an Iraqi's" head and threatening to murder him, gained the information he sought about an insurgent operation.

What are we to make of such an argument? Aside from the fact that citing only two cases and concluding that "torture works" commits the fallacy of Hasty Generalization, what else is to be said about this argument? It is important to examine it because it is the darling argument of those who support torture.

The best way to refute this is to examine the history of torture, and add to that what contemporary empirical studies tell us about its success, rather than just toss up a few cases in which it did or did not work. Both of these issues are addressed by Alfred W. McCoy, in his study *A Question of Torture*. Regarding history, McCoy examines the French experience in Algiers, demonstrating three things: individual torture did not work; mass torture did produce information; but mass torture cost the French the war.[54] The reason for the latter was "in large part because its systematic torture delegitimized the wider war effort in the eyes of most Algerians and many French."[55] McCoy quotes British and French historians and French Generals and Colonels who were part of the French torture program in Algiers.

Regarding the empirical studies, McCoy makes the following statement:

Testing has found that professional interrogators perform within the 45 to 60 percent range in distinguishing truth from lies—little better than flipping a coin.[56]

In other words, even if you arrest someone you believe has pertinent information, you cannot tell if they are telling the truth. So you have to torture more people to get more information, and the slide down the slippery slope has begun. The French slid down this slope in Algiers, torturing more and more people, and ended up executing over 3,000 suspected terrorists as part of their torture program.[57] The Americans found the same thing in Vietnam, through their Phoenix program, where over half the Vietcong captured, tortured and/or killed were not even party members.[58]

As a result of these experiences, even the contemporary U.S. Army Field Manual warns against torture: "Revelation of use of torture by US personnel will bring discredit upon the US and its armed forces while undermining domestic and international support for the war effort."[59]

So torture does not generally work, even if one can craft a few cases in which some information was gleaned from it. To conjure up a case or two, or even a few, and to conclude from that that "torture works," is to commit the fallacy of hasty generalization. Even if supporters of torture succeeded at making the moral case for it, the number of people that would have to tortured in order to win a war, especially a war on terrorism, would be morally prohibitively high. No one can make the Golden Rule say "torture everyone," no matter how hard one twists it in the direction of Yerushalmi. Thus, the argument Yerushalmi makes in favor of torture has far too many problems within it to prove his thesis. Most of all, his argument attempts to support his statist philosophy, in that he believes that rights come from the legal mechanism of the state. The ignorance of the distinction between human rights and civil rights demonstrated in his statism is alarming in itself, since the existence of the state is taken to be morally prior to that of the individual. It is also the belief that allows him to twist the Golden Rule out of its meaning and into a legitimization of hurting others. But in doing so, Yerushalmi shows his hand, and the real issue arises: torture is a state device, not a device of individuals, so if the state feels threatened by a people, any people, it can exercise its power over them in any way it wants to in order to maintain its existence. The only greater power a state could exercise to oppress persons is torture combined with summary execution. Contrary to Yerushalmi's assertions, not even execution alone is as degrading to the person as is breaking him or her down physically and psychologically before killing them. The reason is that torture is a long process of dehumanizing action, not a single one. In fact, the connection between torture and murder is very close, as we have seen by the history of the connection of torture to execution.

The arguments that are frequently given in support of torture are usually a combination of two parts: a utilitarian method and a notion of a common good that is usually defined as the existence of the state. We can see these both at work in the defense of torture made by Mirko Bagaric, professor of law and head of the Deakin Law School.

Bagaric nuances the Yerushalmi argument. His thesis is that torture is permissible where the evidence suggests that this is the only means, due to the immediacy of the situation, to save the life of an innocent person. His reason: it is analogous to the right to self-defense, which is an inviolable right.[60]

The first part of his argument can be summarized in a single sentence: "Given the choice between inflicting a relatively small level of harm on a wrongdoer and saving an innocent person, it is verging on moral indecency to prefer the interests of the wrongdoer." For example, we can conceive of a hostage-taking situation in which one is directly and immediately threatening the life of their hostage which permits killing the hostage-taker if one can get "a clear shot."

Bagaric maintains that there is no logical or moral difference between this hostage scenario and one in which there is "overwhelming evidence that a wrongdoer has kidnapped an innocent person and informs police that the victim will be killed by a co-defender if certain demands are not met." Because it is universally accepted that it is permissible to take the life of the hostage-taker in the first instance, how can it be wrong to violate an even less important right (the right to physical integrity) by torturing the aggressor in the second case in order to save a life? In other words, the argument of Bagaric is that torture of a person is less of a moral offense against him/her than killing him/her.

The analogy fails to point out the fact that in the first case (the "clear shot" one) it is certain that taking a life of a hostage-taker will result in saving the life of an innocent abductee, whereas torture will not necessarily result in this happy ending. Bagaric rejects this response by stating that the same situation occurs with the hostage-taker scenario as well because their gun might in fact be empty, so that they did not pose a real threat to the hostage. Yet we may morally shoot anyway based on the facts we have. In other words, just like we did not know the gun was not loaded, so we do not know if we will get information from torture. But just as we are permitted to shoot the hostage-taker in order to procure the safety of an innocent, so we may torture another in order to procure the safety of other innocents [i.e. citizens].

But shooting is not the same as torturing them. What Bagaric and other supporters of torture fail to realize is that brutalizing another human being effects far more harm on him or her than simply killing them does, both in the short and long term. It also affects the torturer, deepening an inhumane character. It is for these reasons and others like them that torture is deemed by most people and nations to be equally if not more barbaric and morally reprehensible than murder.

What the argument attempts to do is kill the moral weight of a universal ban on torture by forcing it to die the death of a thousand hypothetical nuances. The "might" of an empty gun scenario is highly unlikely in a hostage-taking episode. The "might" of not getting intended information is highly probable. Thus, the qualification fails to make the intended analogy (i.e. it is a false analogy) due to its highly abstract, hypothetical, unlikely, and implausible nature.

Furthermore, in the second case (i.e. the "informing" hostage-taker) one is using the most dehumanizing treatment possible in order to potentially procure a release of a person who may or may not be killed, from a person who may or may not provide needed information to release the kidnapped person. He rejects this response on the grounds that a society that favors the interest of the wrongdoers over the innocent dehumanizes the society even more. But this is not a preferential treatment scenario; it is a case in which rights are said to apply to all equally, irrespective of what they have done. That rights may be curtailed is clear, but that the most basic human right of all—that of personal, psychological, and bodily integrity—may not be abused simply for the sake of gaining information about another. Without that right to human dignity (i.e. not to be tortured) firmly in place, there are no other rights that can be protected, let alone preferred. In other words, if the physical and psychological integrity of a person is not sacrosanct—indeed, if they are not the very basis of the rights to liberty and equality, or at least intimately tied up with these well-recognized rights—then neither liberty nor equality can exist inalienably nor be protected.

The overall problem with such utilitarian scenarios as the arguments of Yerushalmi and Bagaric is that the "ticking time bomb" scenario they all lay out as a 'clear case" of permissible torture almost never occurs, and when it does there are so many evidentiary requirements that must be met that it is an implausible and impractical example. For example, the police would have to know that a bomb has in fact been set to explode at a specific and certain location; that there is in fact no other way to obtain information about it except through torture; that the bomb is about to detonate; that the suspect has in fact all the knowledge that they need to defuse it and that he or she will surrender that knowledge in a very short time if torture is applied.[61]

Perhaps the most critical problem for these pro-torture arguments is that they all presume that our legal and governmental institutions can make the necessary determinations about when torture is called for and permissible, and most importantly that they can control it. But since the legislative and judicial branches of our own government in the U.S. have failed to challenge President Bush when he has claimed such powers for himself, there is every reason to doubt that allowing torture will be controllable and controlled by our government.[62]

What they are attempting to do is to find a wedge to drive into the universal prohibition on human rights violations by torture. But their examples are extreme and implausible and do not meet the demand for the high moral criteria needed to overturn a near-universal prohibition: the prohibition against torture.

One hastens to add that the Founders of this country held that an absolute ban on torture was the trademark of a free democratic government. For example, the Eighth Amendment forbidding "cruel and unusual punishment" directly followed England's lead in proscribing torture. In contradistinction to this, those who support torture do so in order to solve the problem of how to protect innocent lives against terrorist attacks such as 9/11. But the legal mechanisms are all in place for doing just that, and thanks to the PATRIOT Act, the Feds have far more power than they need to stop terrorist attacks without those who support torture having to invent such implausible and tortured scenarios to attempt to justify their position. Torture is not only unneeded, but violates a fundamental value of democracy: the dignity of the human person. Without this principle firmly in place, there is no democracy worth protecting. Democracies die where people's rights are not respected by their government.

In essence then, the utilitarian scenarios that attempt to wedge open the absolute prohibition on torture are as unrealistic as their arguments are immoral. It is a sign of the times that lawyers like Yerushalmi and Bagaric can twist the language of our most deeply held moral principles and use them for reasons that they were formulated to stand against. Their arguments are vacuous and we should never consider lifting the ban on torture that every civilized nation continues to uphold even in fighting terror.

Notes

1. See Philippa Foot, "The Problem of Abortion and the Doctrine of Double Effect," *Virtues and Vices* (Berkeley and Los Angeles: University of California Press, 1978, pgs. 19—32.

2. For more on this, see Alison McIntyre, "Doing Away with Double Effect," *Ethics*, January, 2001. pg. 251.

3. Bentham, Jeremy. *An Introduction to the Principles of Morals and Legislation*, Chapter VIII, "Of Intentionality," n. 6, p. 86.

4. For more on this, see the studies by Stanley Milgram, Obedience to Authority (New York: Harper and Row), 1974. For some of the original work in this area that remains relevant today, see also Solomon Asch, "Opinions and Social Pressure," *Scientific American*, November, 1955.

5. Myers, David G. *Social Psychology* (Boston: McGraw-Hill, 2005), p. 297.

6. Coates, C.A.J. *The Ethics of War* (New York: Manchester University Press, 1997), pgs. 244—245.

7. Walzer, *Just and Unjust Wars*, p. 155.

8. Ibid, p. 156

9. Ibid., p. 157.

10. Niko Price, "Iraq to Stop Counting Civilian Deaad," *Associated Press*, December 10, 2003.

11. For more, see Michael Schwartz, "Is the United States Killing 10,000 Iraqis Every Month? Or is it More?" www.alternet.org, July 6, 2007.

12. Jonathan Bor, "654,000 Deaths Tied to Iraq War," *Baltimore Sun*, October 11, 2006.

13. Tim McGirk, "Collateral Damage or Civilian Massacre in Haditha?" *Time*, March 19, 2006.

14 "Massacre in Haditha: Eight Marines Charged with Killing 24 Iraqis," *Democracy Now*, December 22, 2006.

15. Marjorie Cohn, "Aggressive War: Supreme International Crime," www.truthout.org, November 9, 2004.

16. Helen Thomas, "Attack on Fallujah can't be Justified," *Hearst Newspapers*, November 12, 2004.

17. Rory McCarthy, "U.S. Denies Need for Fallujah Aid Convoy," *The Guardian U.K.*, November 15, 2004.

18. "U.S. Broadcast Exclusive: "Fallujah: The Hidden Massacre' on the U.S. Use of Napalm-like White Phosphorus Bombs," *Democracy Now*, November 8, 2005.

19. Walzer, Michael, *Just and Unjust Wars*, p. 187.

20. For more, see Dahr Jamal, "Countless My Lai Massacres in Iraq," www.truthout.org, May 30, 2006. See also Aaron Glantz and Alaa Hassan, "U.S. Miltary Hides Many More Hadithas," *Inter-Press Service*, June 7, 2006.

74   The Ethical Case against the Conduct of the Invasion and Occupation of Iraq

See also Patrick Cockburn, "U.S. Victory against Cult Leader was 'Massacre'," *The Independent/U.K.*, January 31, 2007.

21. Dahr Jamal and Ali al-Fadhily, "Official Lies Over Najaf Battle Exposed," *Inter-Press Service*, February 1, 2007.

22. Chris Hedges & Laila Al-Arian, "The Other War; Iraq Vets Bear Witness," *The Nation*, June 30, 2007.

23. Michael Hirsh and John Barry, "The Salvador Option," *Newsweek*, January 8, 2005.

24. Geoffrey Lean and Severin Carrell, "U.S. Prepares to Use Toxic Gases in Iraq," *The U.K. Independent*," March 2, 2003.

25. For these and other stories concerning U.S. arrest, detention, and torture of journalists, see Reporters Without Borders, at www.rsf.org. See also Naomi Klein, "You Asked for my Evidence, Mr. Ambassador. Here it is," *The Guardian U.K.*, December 4, 2004; Luke Harding, "U.S. Military 'Brutalized' Journalists," *The Guardian U.K.*, January 13, 2004.

26. See Bert DeBelder, "Four Years into the Occupation: No Health for Iraq," *Global Policy Forum*, March 21, 2007; see also "Armed Groups Occupy Hospitals and Kidnap Doctors," *Global Policy Forum*, February 13, 2007.

27. Colonel Dan Smith, "Beyond Nuremberg: Crimes Against Peace," *Counterpunch*, August 11, 2006.

28. Neil A. Lewis, "ACLU Presents Accusations of Serious Abuse of Iraqi Civilians," *The New York Times*, January 25, 2005.

29. John Hendren, "Pentagon Files Reveal More Allegations of Abuse in Iraq," *The Los Angeles Times*, January 25, 2005.

30. "Iraq War a 'Jihadist Cause Celebre," *Aljazeera*, September 27, 2006. Cited from www.aljazeera.com.

31. From the Taguba report, but also quoted in Seymour Hersh, "Torture at Abu Ghraib," *The New Yorker*, May 10, 2004.

32. See the Human Rights Watch Report, *The Road to Abu Ghraib*, pgs. 12—18, June, 2004.

33. Mark Danner, "The Logic of Torture," *The New York Review of Books*, June 24, 2004.

34. Ibid. See also Brian Whitaker, "American Troops are Killing and Abusing Afghans, Rights Body Says," *The Guardian*, March 8, 2004.

35. Ibid.

36. Suzanne Goldenberg, Tania Branigan and Vikram Dodd, "Guantanamo Abuse Same as Abu Ghraib, say Britons," *The Guardian U.K.*, May 14, 2004.

37. Marjorie Cohn, "Redefining Torture," *Truthout*, January 3, 2005.

38. Ibid.

39. Andrew Cockburn, "How Rumsfeld Micromanaged Torture," *Counterpunch*, March 1—5, 2007.

40. S. 3930, "The Military Commissions Act of 2006," sec. III, subsection VII, sec. 8.

41. One example of the many psychological studies that reach this conclusion: *Archives of General Psychiatry*, 2007 (from *Los Angeles Times*, "Psychological Torture Just as Bad, Study Finds," March 6).

42. From Amnesty International, www.amnesty.org.

43. Andrew Sullivan, "Soyster Speaks," The Atlantic, December 11, 2007.

44. Alfred W. McCoy, "The Hidden History of CIA Torture," www.tomdispatch.com, September 10, 2004. McCoy later expanded this article in a book entitled *A Question of Torture: CIA Interrogation, from the Cold War to the War on Terror*, 2006, Henry Holt and Company, New York.

45. My choice of Yerushalmi and Bagaric is largely because an excellent discussion of Dershowitz and Ignatieff is done by Alfred W. McCoy, *A Question of Torture* (New York: Metropolitan Books, 2006), pgs. 177—ff. Also, Ignatieff has recanted his support of torture, so analyzing his previous arguments favoring torture would not contribute much to the discussion.

46. Yerushalmi, David, "On Torture," *Intellectual Conservative*, October 4, 2006.

47. Walzer, *Just and Unjust Wars*, p. 252.

48. Ibid., p. 253.

49. See, for example, A.W. Kruglanski & S. Fishman, "The Psychology of Terrorism: Syndrome versus tool perspective," *Journal of Terrorism and political Violence*, 2006. See also the study by Robert Pape, written in abbreviated form, in "Dying to Kill Us," *New York Times*, September 22, 2003.

50. Ibid.

51. Ronald Dworkin, *Taking Rights Seriously* (Cambridge: Harvard University Press, 1977), p. 28.

52. In this, I am following Lon Fuller, who argues that laws have a normative content, and Ronald Dworkin, who uses Fuller's understanding of legal process to develop a rights-based account of law. See Lon Fuller, "The Forms and Limits of Adjudication," *Harvard Law Review*, 92 (1978), and Ronald Dworkin, *Taking Rights Seriously* (Cambridge: Harvard University Press, 1978), p. 105—130. See also Dworkin, *Law's Empire* (Oxford, 1998), especially Chapters 2 & 6.

53. Jay S. Bybee, Memorandum for Alberto R. Gonzales, August 1, 2002. www.news.findlaw.com/nytimes/docs/doj/bybee80102mem.pdf

54. McCoy, op. cit., pgs. 18—20; 195—200.

55. Ibid., p. 199.

56. Ibid., pgs. 194—195.

57. Ibid., pgs. 195—196.

58. Ibid., pg. 199.

59. FM 43-52, Intelligence Interrogation (Washington, Department of the Army, September 28, 1992), pgs. 1—8. Quoted in McCoy, p. 200.

60. Bagaric, Mirko, "A Case for Torture," www.theage.com. The web version is an abbreviated form of a longer paper to be published by the University of San Francisco Law Review.

61. This was first made clear by William Schultz, Executive Director of U.S. section of Amnesty International.

62. This also makes the argument given by Alan Dershowitz for the moral permissibility of torture provided a warrant is obtained, a dubious argument if not a completely vacuous one.

Chapter Five
International Law and the Invasion of Iraq

It is fair to state that there are clear moral principles underlying the law of war. For *jus ad bellum* concerns in Just War Theory, there exists the United Nations Charter which defines just cause and proper authority in agreed-upon articles. For *jus in bello*, there are the Geneva Conventions, the Hague Conventions, and the Nuremberg Principles, among others, defining what constitutes proper and improper behavior in war, and dealing with the Just War issues of Discrimination and Proportionality.

An interesting question immediately arises concerning the relationship between the Just War Theory and international law. Do Just War principles undergird international law or did international law overtake and replace Just War Theory as the basis for war and its conduct? Since the same categories of the analysis of war are covered in international law as in Just War Theory, and since the former is the latecomer on the scene, I want to argue that international law has largely taken over the role of deliberation concerning war, but that the ethical principles and constraints discussed in Just War Theory are presupposed by international law and inform the latter discipline. Therefore, Just War Theory is not and cannot be "outmoded," since it is the foundation of our international law dialogues concerning the issues of war, and in fact is mixed in with the legal discussions. Put most succinctly, the position taken here is that the principles and restraints which have for centuries been discussed under the ethical auspices of "Just War Theory" now find their clearest and most widely accepted and functional expression in the international laws of war. A clear cut distinction between the morality and legality of war, then, cannot be made. Michael Walzer also places them together under the title "The War Convention," but he clearly maintains the same idea put forth here:

> the legal handbooks are not the only place to find the war convention, and its actual existence is demonstrated not by the existence of the handbooks but by the moral arguments that everywhere accompany the practice of war. The common law of combat is developed through a kind of practical casuistry.[1]

The *jus ad bellum* in International Law

We begin then, with the notion of just cause in international law. The U.N. Charter stipulates in two different articles what the legal understanding of just cause is to be:

Article 2(4): "All members shall refrain in their international relations from the threat or use of force against the territorial integrity or political independence of any state or in any other manner inconsistent with the purposes of the United Nations."

Article 51: "Nothing in the present Charter shall impair the inherent right of individual or collective self-defense if an armed attack occurs against a member of the United Nations, until the Security Council has taken the measures necessary to maintain international peace and security."

Many international lawyers add to the understanding of Article 51 the Just War condition that if an attack is imminent, the nation going to war may bypass U.N. Security Council authorization.

There is also the issue of aggression, related to just cause in that it is a direct violation of it:

Article 39: "The Security Council shall determine the existence of any threat to the peace, breach of the peace, or act of aggression and shall make recommendations or decide what measure shall be taken in accordance with Articles 41 and 42, to maintain or restore international peace and security."

Article 41: "The Security Council may decide what measures not involving the use of armed force are to be employed to give effect to its decisions, and it may call upon the Members of the United Nations to apply such measures. These may include complete or partial interruption of economic relations and of rail, sea, air, postal, telegraphic, radio, and other means of communication, and the severance of diplomatic relations."

Article 42: "Should the Security Council consider that measures provided for in Article 41 would be inadequate or have proved to be inadequate, it may take such action by air, sea, or land forces as may be necessary to maintain or restore international peace and security. Such action may include demonstrations, blockade, and other operations by air, sea, or land forces of Members of the United Nations."

Adding to the law concerning aggression, there is also the *Report of the Special Committee on the Question of Defining Aggression*, presented to the U.N. General Assembly (1974). In that report, the definition of aggression is presented in Article 1:

> Aggression is the use of armed force by a State against the sovereignty, territorial integrity or political independence of another State, or in any other manner inconsistent with the Charter of the United Nations, as set out in this definition.

Finally, the Nuremberg Military Tribunal condemned aggression as "the supreme international crime."

The question that immediately rises is the one concerning how to interpret these Articles. Although we cannot involve ourselves in the lawyerly discussions of interpretation, we can acknowledge that there is a certain ambiguity contained in the laws, as there are in the principles of restraint we call Just War Theory.[2]

Concomitant with our discussion of just cause, we have also answered the question of proper authority: international law requires a nation considering going to war to obtain the approval of the U.N. Security Council before proceeding, unless it is being attacked or under threat of imminent attack.

How did the United States fare in applying this to the wars in Afghanistan and Iraq? Since these are two wars, we must engage in two separate analyses. If it is true that the attackers of the U.S. on 9/11 were members of the Al Qaeda terrorist network based in Afghanistan, and the de facto government of that country, the Taliban, deliberately supported and gave shelter to the organization members in order to prevent them from being brought to justice, the attack on Afghanistan could perhaps be justified by international law standards, provided the U.S. was willing to work with the International Court of Justice. However, there is sufficient reason to doubt all of these premises. Thus, the just cause criterion of the Just War Theory and of international law has likely not been met. First, the FBI does not have the 9/11 attackers posted on their web site, because they state that the evidence is lacking for putting him there as the culprit for 9/11. Here is the salient quote from the reporter who first noticed that no mention of bin Laden involving 9/11 has ever been placed on the FBI web site. He had interviewed Rex Tomb, Chief of Investigative Publicity for the FBI.

> When asked why there is no mention of 9/11 on Bin Laden's *Most Wanted* web page, Tomb said, "The reason why 9/11 is not mentioned on Usama Bin Laden's Most Wanted page is because the FBI has no *hard evidence* connecting Bin Laden to 9/11.[3]

Second, the Taliban in fact offered to turn over Al Qaeda members to the international court of justice. The U.S. refused to accept this offer.[4] Third, it is a plausible argument that the criterion of proper authority was not met, as the United Nations did not sanction the U.S. attack on Afghanistan, called "Operation Enduring Freedom." Those who maintain that the U.S. did not need the approval of the U.N. would have to argue that this attack was a response to an attack on the U.S., in which case the attack on Afghanistan would come under the right to collective self-defense, as permitted by Article 51 of the U.N. Charter. If there are significant doubts concerning whether the attack was done by Al Qaeda, then this defense becomes moot.

The attack on Iraq, however, was done under different pretenses than Afghanistan, and thus must be analyzed separately from the case of Afghanistan. Although the public and the corporate media generally group both attacks under the umbrella phrase "the war on terrorism," they only loosely fit together in this way. This is shown when one goes through the moral and legal analysis of each.

There have been several articulate cases made to cast doubt on the arguments of those who maintain that a U.S. attack on Iraq is covered under UNC Article 51. One of the most significant is the article "The Myth of Preemptive Self-Defense," by Mary Ellen O'Connell, Professor of Law at The Ohio State University. The other noteworthy ones are from the Center for Economic and Social Rights, "Tearing up the Rules: The Illegality of Invading Iraq," and the letter to U.N. Secretary General Kofi Anan by the organization Lawyers Against the War. I will rely on primarily on the O'Connell paper to synopsize the application of the laws of war to the U.S. invasion of Iraq, for the reason that she presents counter-arguments to the case against the legality of U.S. actions, and refutes them.

Regarding just cause and proper authority with Iraq, O'Connell begins as we did above, with U.N. Charter Articles 2(4) and 51, and concludes that the U.S. committed violations of international law with the invasion of Iraq. Regarding 2(4), Professor Anthony D'Amato counters that Article 2(4) is only a prohibition on force aimed at the territorial integrity and political independence of states. O'Connell responds that the U.N. Security Council passed a unanimous resolution condemning the Israeli bombing of Iraq's Osirik nuclear plant, which "helped solidify the general understanding that Article 2(4) is a general prohibition on force."[5] This understanding is opposed to the conservative argument in favor of attacking Iraq, represented by D'Amato's narrow interpretation of 2(4).

Applying Article 51, O'Connell goes on to state that "an attack must be underway or must have already occurred in order to trigger the right of unilateral self-defense."[6] The International Court of Justice upheld this interpretation in 1986 in the case *Nicaragua v. U.S.* Today, the Bush Doctrine of preventive war counts as just cause for war "striking an enemy even in the absence of specific evidence of a coming attack," or even the alleged violation of a disarmament requirement.[7] Both of these issues were rejected as *casus belli* by the International Court of Justice in an advisory opinion.[8] Again, the unanimous condemnation by the U.N.S.C. of the Israeli bombing of Osirik is cited by O'Connell as a case in point.

The counter argument presented by O'Connell is from Professor Louis Henkin, who argues that Article 51 provides an "inherent" right to anticipatory self-defense. O'Connell counters with an extended rebuttal, specifically that Henkin's position "is fundamentally at odds with the Charter's design." Aside from the fact that this "requires privileging the word 'inherent' over the plain terms of Article 2(4), an important reason for rejecting this kind of interpretation is that "it is an exception that would overthrow the prohibition on the use of force in Article 2(4) and thus the very purposes of the U.N."[9] This is because when there is a lack of evidence of an armed attack, Article 2(4) requires multilateral decision-making, not that of a single nation-state.

O'Connell acknowledges that the pro-invasion defenders leaned heavily on UNSC Resolution 678 (1990) as providing continuing authorization to use force against Iraq until international peace and security are restored. However, the defenders neglect to mention that Resolution 687 terminated the use of force authorization by declaring that "a formal cease-fire is effective between Iraq and Kuwait and member states."

We can extend this line of counter-argument to those who would use any UNSC resolution to justify an attack on Iraq. When the Security Council authorizes force, it does so quite clearly, usually by using the phrase "all necessary means." It did not do so on any other resolution concerning Iraq; not even the oft-cited Resolution 1441, in which it threatens 'serious consequences" of any "material breach" of past resolutions by Iraq. The United States had to take it upon itself to make this judgment in order to justify its attack on Iraq, and that is beyond its proper authority, as we have seen.

The *jus in bello* in International Law

We now turn to international law of *jus in bello*. In this analysis, we will refer to five areas of international law concerning the conduct of war: the Charter of the International Military Tribunal at Nuremberg; the First Geneva Conventions; the Geneva Convention Protocols; the Third Geneva Convention; and the Convention against Torture.

The *Charter of the International Military Tribunal at Nuremberg*

Section II, Article 6, presents the definition of international crimes "coming within the jurisdiction of the Tribunal" as the following:

(a) "Crimes Against Peace: namely, planning, preparation, initiation or waging of a war of aggression, or a war in violation of international treaties, agreements or assurances, or participation in a common plan or conspiracy for the accomplishment of any of the foregoing."

(b) "War Crimes: namely, violations of the laws or customs of war. Such violations shall include, but not be limited to, murder, ill-treatment or deportation to slave labor or for any other purpose of civilian population of or in occupied territory, murder or ill-treatment of prisoners of war or persons on the seas, killing of hostages, plunder of public or private property, wanton destruction of cities, towns or villages, or devastation not justified by military necessity."

(c) "Crimes against humanity: namely, murder, extermination, enslavement, deportation, and other inhumane acts committed against any civilian population, before or during the war,; or persecutions on political, racial or religious grounds in execution of or in connection with any crime within the jurisdiction of the Tribunal, whether or not in violation of the domestic law of the country where perpetrated."

"Leaders, organizers, instigators and accomplices participating in the formulation or execution of a common plan or conspiracy to commit any of the foregoing crimes are responsible for all acts performed by any persons in execution of such plan."

Article 7 stipulates that Heads of State "shall not be considered as [exempt] from responsibility or mitigating punishment."

Article 8 continues in the same line and states that "the fact that the Defendant acted pursuant to order of his Government or of a superior shall not free him from responsibility."

We have already seen some of the number of horrific acts that were approved by Bush cabinet members and set into motion by generals and then actually performed by soldiers on the civilians or Iraq to see the war crimes that have been committed in our names. We will see more as this chapter progresses. Taken together, these instances should be sufficient to demonstrate that the war has not been fought justly by these standards alone. But let us continue our *in bello* analysis.

The Geneva Conventions

It is not an understatement to say that the United States has violated a large number of the Geneva Conventions in its occupation of Iraq. Such a case cannot be fully made here due to the number of Articles of the Convention that have been violated. However, some of the more important violations will be outlined here.

Geneva Convention IV (1949) concerns the *Protection of Civilian Persons in Time of War*.

That the Conventions apply unequivocally to the United States is not only clear from the fact that the U.S. is a signatory to the Convention (as is Iraq), but from the fact that it is explicitly stated in Part I, Article 2:

In addition to the provisions which shall be implemented in peace-time, the present Convention shall apply to all cases of declared war or of any other armed conflict which may arise between two or more other High Contracting Parties, even if the state of war is not recognized by one of them. The Convention shall also apply to all cases of partial or total occupation of the territory of a High Contracting Part, even if the said occupation meets with no armed resistance.

So who is protected by the Convention? Article 3 states that

Persons taking no active part in the hostilities, including members of armed forces who have laid down their arms and those placed hors de combat by sickness, wounds, detention, or any other cause, shall in all circumstances by treated humanely, without any adverse distinction founded on race, colour, religion or faith, sex, birth or wealth, or any other similar criteria.

Here are the parts of the Convention by which one can make the case that the United States has illegally conducted the war on Iraq:

First, the U.S. has directly attacked hospitals in violation of the Convention. Part II, Article 18 states that "Civilian hospitals organized to give care to the wounded and sick, the infirm and maternity cases, may in no circumstances be the object of attack but shall at all times be respected and protected by the Parties to the conflict."

We have already documented the incidents at Fallujah and numerous other cities, in which the U.S. directly bombed a hospital and refused to allow civilian humanitarian organizations such as the Red Crescent access to the city after the civilians were directly attacked.

Second, with regard to the treatment of protected persons under the Convention, Part III, Article 31 states that "No physical or moral coercion shall be exercised against protected persons, in particular to obtain information from them or from third parties." Article 32 is even stronger in its wording regarding this issue:

> The High Contracting Parties specifically agree that each of them is prohibited from taking any measure of such a character as to cause the physical suffering or extermination of protected persons in their hands. This prohibition applies not only to murder, torture, corporal punishments, mutilation and medical or scientific experiments not necessitated by the medical treatment of a protected person, but also to any other measures of brutality whether applied by civilian or military agents.

We have already examined just a few of the noted instances of torture that have been occurring at numerous locations controlled and maintained by the United States. That the actions engaged in such places as Abu Ghraib, Guantanamo Bay, and various other locations in Iraq and Afghanistan are direct violations of the Geneva Conventions can be asserted here without further elaboration. But for more information, one might consult the Human Rights Watch (HRW) report entitled "Enduring Freedom: Abuses by U.S. Forces in Afghanistan (2004)," in which numerous cases of abuse of detainees have been documented at various sites in Afghanistan, including "extreme sleep deprivation, exposure to freezing temperatures, and severe beatings." The various places documented by HRW in Afghanistan where these activities are occurring include Bagram airbase, Kabul, Kandahar, Jalalabad, and Asadabad. Bagram alone was the scene of four to five deaths by torture. The same situation was reported in Abu Ghraib by HRW as well. The American Civil Liberties Union has obtained 44 autopsy reports of detainees in Iraq and Afghanistan, and has concluded that all 44, as well as a summary of other autopsy reports of detainees in both countries, were all the direct result of U.S. interrogation methods. Twenty-one of the 44 deaths were homicides.[10]

Further, Part III, Section III, Article 76, and Section IV, in its entirety, specifically regulates the treatment of detainees by requiring occupying powers to "be detained in the occupied country, and if convicted . . . serve their sentences therein," along with the right to receive medical attention, spiritual assistance (Article 76), live in cells protected against the rigors of climate, dampness, and heat, as well as adequate ventilation and lighting, and with sanitary facilities "for their use, day and night" (Article 85). Significantly, the Convention takes great pains to specify in detail, in a separate section covering numerous Articles (105-116), the rights of the detainees to communicate with the outside world. In Afghanistan and Iraq, the ICRC has access to only a few of the U.S. controlled sites where detainees are being held, according to the HRW report. None of the published reports on detainee conditions has failed to underscore the fact that these conditions have not been met by U.S. (detainee) prisons.

Geneva Convention Protocols

Continuing with this theme, Additional Protocol I of the *Geneva Conventions*, Part III, Article 35, limits the use of types of weaponry:

> It is prohibited to employ weapons, projectiles and material and methods of warfare of a nature to cause superfluous injury or unnecessary suffering.

As if to test that law, there have been several weapons the U.S. has reportedly used in Iraq which are directly designed to cause immense suffering and even death at the end of that suffering. For example, one device being used is a small megaphone that can "emit a piercing tone so excruciating to humans, its boosters say, that it causes crowds to disperse, clears buildings and repels intruders. . . . It will knock [some people] on their knees." It is also possible that this weapon can produce permanent hearing loss or even cellular damage.[11]

Next, there have been charges coming out of Iraq that the United States has been using laser weapons which incinerate various sections of the body without piercing the skin or damaging the surroundings. The same claim is being made for alleged U.S. microwave weapons.[12]

Article 35 continues with a ban on weapons "which are intended, or may be intended, to cause widespread, long-term and severe damage to the natural environment." In direct violation of this Article, the U.S. uses depleted uranium (DU) in its bombs and shell casings, which in turn spread intense radiation into the soil, water, and buildings around them. This was first done in the 1991 Gulf War, and is continuing today in Iraq. The results have been nothing short of stunning:[13]

- Eight out of twenty men who served in one unit in the 2003 invasion of Iraq now have malignancies. That means that 40% of the soldiers in that unit have developed malignancies in just 16 months.
- Those who develop malignancies that quickly can expect to develop multiple cancers, as attested by studies from the results of the NATO use of DU in the former Yugoslavia.
- Out of 580,000 soldiers who served in the first Gulf War in 1991, 11,000 are dead, and by 2000 there were 325,000 on permanent medical disability.
- The number of disabled vets has been increasing by 43,000 every year.
- Women who have had sexual intercourse with men who served in the Gulf War that resulted in pregnancy, have a significantly high number of babies born with birth defects. In a group of 251 soldiers from a study group in Mississippi who had had normal babies prior to the Gulf War, 67% had deformed babies after the war. They were born with missing legs, arms, organs or eyes.
- DU weapons have been sold by the U.S. to 29 countries, including Israel, who used them in the Yom Kippur war in 1973.
- Today, 42 of the 50 United States are contaminated with DU from manufacture, testing, and deployment.

In addition, today in Afghanistan, the urine samples show the highest level of uranium ever recorded by a civilian population. Test results have been analyzed for a number of possible causes, but they all point to the same source: use of DU by U.S. forces.[14]

Although Secretary of Defense Donald Rumsfeld and Attorney General Alberto Gonzalez have attempted to bypass the Geneva Conventions by designating captured prisoners as "enemy combatants" rather than as "prisoners of war," that designation itself is forbidden under international law, specifically by Article 45 of the Additional Protocol:[15]

Section 1: "A person who takes part in hostilities and falls into the power of an adverse Party shall be presumed to be a prisoner of war, and therefore shall be protected by the Third Convention . . . Should any doubt arise as to whether any such person is entitled to the status of prisoner of war, he shall continue to have such status and, therefore, to be protected by the Third Convention of this Protocol until such time as his status has been determined by a competent tribunal."

Section 2: "If a person who has fallen into the power of an adverse Party is not held as a prisoner of war and is to be tried by the Party for an offence arising out of the hostilities, he shall have the right to assert his entitlement to prisoner-of-war status before a judicial tribunal and to have that question adjudicated."

So we can see that the United States, by refusing to grant the status of POW to the detainees, by refusing them the ability to claim that status, and by refusing them the right of adjudication of that title, is committing three ongoing counts of direct violations of international law.

With regard to the civilian population, Part IV of the Additional Protocol sets very strict parameters.

First, Article 48, "Basic rule," requires that "Parties to the conflict shall at all times distinguish between the civilian population and combatants and between civilian objects and military objectives." Further, Article 50 states that "the presence within the civilian population of individuals who do not come within the definition of civilians does not deprive the population of its civilian character." Therefore, "acts or threats of violence the primary purpose of which is to spread terror among the civilian population are prohibited" (Article 51, Section 2). The article continues by banning all *"indiscriminate"* strikes on civilians, including an attack on a whole city in which one or more military targets are located, and an attack violating the rules of *proportionality* between civilian casualties and military objective (Article 51, Section 5).

In other words, there may be *no direct attacks on civilians of any means and for any purpose.* Any failure to abide by those limits is a violation of international law.

But the actual stories from the soldiers returning tell us that there is massive violation of the laws of the Geneva Conventions and Protocols regarding the treatment of civilians going on in Afghanistan and Iraq. *The Nation* magazine interviewed fifty combat veterans of the 2003 Iraq invasion from around the U.S. Published on July 30, 2007, the interviews show clear patterns of slaughters of Iraqi civilians, many of them women and children. This was reinforced by the report from Human Rights Watch called "Hearts and Minds: Post-war Civilian Deaths in Baghdad Caused by U.S. Forces." Together, they make for not only compelling reading, but for an open and shut case regarding United States violation of the ethical norms of *jus in bello* and of the Geneva Conventions and Protocol concerning treatment of civilians. Here is a sampling of the stories the returning soldiers told *The Nation* interviewers.[16]

1) Specialist Michael Harmon: "An IED [improvised explosive device] went off, the gun-happy soldiers just started shooting anywhere and the baby got hit. And this baby looked at me . . . like asking me. . . . Why do I have a bullet in my leg? I was just like, This is it. This is ridiculous."

2) "Veterans described reckless firing once they left their compounds. Some shot holes into cans of gasoline being sold along the roadside and then tossed grenades into the pools of gas to set them ablaze. Others opened fire on children. These shootings often enraged Iraqi witnesses."

3) Veterans talked of lawless raids on the homes of Iraqi citizens, where, "stymied by poor intelligence, [they would] invade neighborhoods where insurgents operate, bursting into homes in the hope of surprising fighters or finding weapons. But such catches, they said, are rare. Far more common were stories in which soldiers assaulted a home, destroyed property in their futile search and left terrorized civilians struggling to repair the damage and begin the long torment of trying to find family members who were hauled away as suspects . . . Physical abuse of Iraqis during raids was common."

4) Tens of thousands of Iraqis—military officials estimate more than 60,000—have been arrested and detained since the beginning of the occupation." Orders were given to detain Iraqis based on their clothes alone. On raids, anyone of military age was taken.

5) Specialist Resta: "We were told from the first second that we arrived there, and this was in writing on the wall in our aid station, that we were not to treat Iraqi civilians unless they were about to die."

6) Supply convoys, operated by KBR (Kellogg, Brown & Root), "often cut through densely populated areas, reaching speeds over sixty miles an hour . . . leapt meridians in traffic jams, ignored traffic signals, swerved without warning onto sidewalks, scattering pedestrians and slammed into civilian vehicles, shoving them off the road. Iraqi civilians, including children, were frequently run over and killed. Veterans said they sometimes shot drivers of civilian cars that moved into convoy formations or attempted to pass convoys as a warning to other drivers to get out of the way. . . . Convoys did not slow down or attempt to brake when civilians inadvertently got in front of their vehicles."

7) "Following an explosion or ambush, soldiers in the heavily armed escort vehicles often fired indiscriminately in a furious effort to suppress further attacks . . . [leaving] many civilians wounded or dead . . . civilians being shot or run over by convoys . . . were so numerous that many were never reported."

8) Patrols "fired often and without much warning on Iraqi civilians in a desperate bid to ward off attacks."

9) Sometimes killing innocent civilians was justified by framing them as terrorists by planting a gun on them after the American troops fired on crowds of unarmed Iraqis.

10) Rules of engagement were often improvised. Staff Sgt. James Zuelow stated that "we were given a long list of stuff and, to be honest, a lot of time we would look at it and throw it away." "Cover your own butt was the first rule of engagement" said Lt. Van Engelen. "There's no such thing as a warning shot" confirmed Specialist Resta.

The Pentagon report on how it deals with civilians in Iraq totaled just two pages.

Geneva Convention III

The Third Geneva Convention deals with treatment of POW's, who by definition include "members of other militias and members of other volunteer corps, including those of organized resistance movements, belonging to a Party to the conflict and operating in or outside their own territory."

Such prisoners are immune from brutal treatment, according to Part III, Section I, Article 17:

> No physical or mental torture, nor any other form of coercion, may be inflicted on prisoners of war to secure from them information of any kind whatever. Prisoners of war who refuse to answer may not be threatened, insulted, or exposed to any unpleasant or disadvantageous treatment of any kind.

The Convention against Torture and Other Cruel, Inhuman or Degrading Treatment or Punishment

Continuing with the torture theme, this Convention defines torture very specifically, and it should be quoted in full:

> For the purposes of this Convention, torture means any act by which severe pain of suffering, whether physical or mental, is intentionally inflicted on a person for such purposes as obtaining from him or a third person information or a confession, punishing him for an act he or a third person has committed or is suspected of having committed, or intimidating or coercing him or a third person, or for any reason based on discrimination of any kind, when such pain or suffering is inflicted by or at the instigation of or with the consent or acquiescence of a public official or other person acting in an official capacity. It does not include pain or suffering arising only from, inherent in or incidental to lawful sanctions.

That the use of torture is itself legally superfluous is seen in Article 15:

> Each State Party shall ensure that any statement which is established to have been made as a result of torture shall not be invoked as evidence in any proceedings, except against a person accused of torture as evidence that the statement was made.

Given the instances we have examined, there can be no doubt that the U.S. is in gross violation of international law on the subject of torture. What is more useful regarding this Convention, though, is the other stipulations it makes concerning torture.

Article 2 states that "no exceptional circumstances whatsoever . . . may be invoked as a justification of torture." Further, "an order from a superior officer or a public authority may not be invoked as a justification of torture."

The conduct of the war in Iraq marks a new low for the world leadership role of the United States. When a nation that is supposed to lead the world in its vision and its adherence to common, nearly universally accepted principles of conduct, flatly refuses to do so on the grounds of its own self-interest and overwhelming immense power, and further looks for ways to justify their presumption that "power exempts from law," it is a nation in serious trouble in terms of its function as a role model for the world, in terms of its own commitment to international cooperation and processes, and perhaps most of all in terms of the principles of morality and the rule of law.

Notes

1. Walzer, *Just and Unjust Wars*, pgs. 44—45.
2. Yehuda Melzer presents an excellent discussion of the problems of interpretation in his book Concepts of Just War (Leyden: A.W. Sitjthoff, 1975).
3. Ed Hass, "FBI Says 'No Hard Evidence Connecting bin Laden to 9/11," *Muckracker Report*, June 6, 2006. If they had no evidence in 2006, they had none in 2001 or 2003. Thanks to Mickey Huff of *Project Censored* for providing this reference.
4. See Rory McCarthy and Julian Borger, "Taliban Ready to Strike a Deal on bin Laden," *Guardian*, February 22, 2001. See also Alexander Cockburn and Jeffrey St. Clair, "How Bush was Offered bin Laden and Blew it," *Counterpunch*, November 1, 2004. While the date of this latter story is later than my stipulated cut-off point regarding legitimate evidence of the March 19, 2003 invasion, I am using it because it highlights the fact that even the American media reported this fact in 2001—e.g. CBS News, on September 25, 2001.
5. Mary Ellen O'Connell, "The Myth of Preemptive Self-Defense," *The American Society of International Law*, August, 2002, p. 5.
6. Ibid.
7. Michael E. O'Hanlon, Susan E. Rice, and James B. Steinberg, "The New National Security Strategy and Preemption," www.brookings.edu/comm/policybriefs/pb113.pdf, January, 2003.
8. 1996 I.C.J. 226, 266. Cited in O'Connell, p. 12.
9. Ibid. p. 13.
10. "U.S. Operatives Killed Detainees During Interrogations in Afghanistan and Iraq," American Civil Liberties Union, October 24, 2005.
11. William M. Arkin, "The Pentagon's Secret Scream," *The Los Angeles Times*, March 8, 2004.
12. "Star Wars in Iraq: Is the U.S. Using New Experimental Tactical High Energy Laser Weapons in Iraq?," *Democracy Now!*," July 25, 2006.
13. Each of these seven facts was reported first by the American Free Press. The list here has been excerpted from the article by Leuren Moret, "Depleted Uranium: Dirty Bombs, Dirty Missiles, Dirty Bullets," *San Francisco Bay View*, August 22, 2004.
14. Mohammed Daud Miraki, "Perpetual Death from America," www.rense.com, February 24, 2003.
15. The now-famous Gonzalez memo, authored in 2002, called the Conventions "quaint," and argued in numerous ways that the U.S. was not obliged to follow them. See Alberto Gonzalez, "Decision Re Application of the Geneva Convention on Prisoners of War to the Conflict with Al Qaeda and the Taliban," January 25, 2002.
16. Chris Hedges & Laila Al-Arian, "The Other War: Iraq Vets Bear Witness," *The Nation*, July 30, 2007.

Chapter Six
Preparing for the Next Deception

The End Game in Iraq

We have analyzed the decision to invade and occupy Iraq and found that decision to be deeply flawed logically, morally, and legally. But now that we have committed ourselves to being there, the obvious question is "what next?"

Robert Fisk, in a recent interview, said this of the U.S. presence in Iraq: "The Americans must leave; the Americans will leave; the Americans can't leave."[1] That adroit analysis sums up very acuity the problem we now face. Many commentators say we must leave but no one knows how. The solutions are as numerous as are the analysts. The "Iraq Study Group," headed by James Baker, suggested a "stay the course" model, including the privatization of Iraqi oil fields. The neocons have painted apocalypse scenarios in the event of U.S. withdrawal from Iraq. But nearly all analysts agree that the invasion was about two things: oil and empire. The U.S. has been building its desire of both for decades, and with the collapse of the Soviet Union in 1991, this is its defining moment. We have seen the plans for empire in the documents of the Project for a New American Century, translated into Bush foreign policy. If the arguments that the U.S. is in Iraq for the oil have been unconvincing, and the recommendations of the Iraq Study Group are unconvincing, two recent news stories should finish the oil argument. First, the Iraqi government is close to passing a new oil law that privatize Iraq oil fields and share the profits one way or another with private (U.S.) oil companies. In addition, the Bush administration, shortly after Baghdad had been occupied, requested an additional $2.1 billion of taxpayer money to rebuild the Iraq oil fields. That this was one of the first requests for extra money, and a sizeable request at that, demonstrates the Bush priorities in invading this sovereign nation.

So oil and empire are clearly U.S. goals. Now, though, we are in a quagmire. If the U.S. withdraws from Iraq, it admits to failure at empire and gives up its quest to control both oil supplies and the Mideast in general. If it stays in Iraq, it continues to suck billions of dollars per year into a black hole of civil war, insurgency, chaos and disorder, a collapsed infrastructure, and a dysfunctional government. The scenario does not look bright in Iraq right now. Hence, the astute observation from Mr. Fisk.

Perhaps the first thing to do is to respond to the doomsday scenarios predicted by the neocons that they say will result from U.S. withdrawal constructed. It is frankly amazing that the very same people who had such rosy predictions about the great consequences that were to come from a U.S. invasion of Iraq, and who were dead wrong on every prediction they made, should be taken seriously in their next set of predictions. One would think their credibility had been severely damaged, but they are still the main voice heard in the corporate media.[2] So what are the disastrous consequences for American withdrawal from Iraq?

Robert Dreyfus, writing for the *Washington Monthly*, had perhaps the most succinct review of neocon dire predictions.[3]

1) The neocons argue that Al Qaeda and other terrorists will take over Iraq if we leave. Dreyfus responds that al Qaeda in Iraq (AQI) comprise only 5-10% of the population. Even if they did come to dominate the Sunni resistance in Iraq, they do not have the muscle to take over Baghdad against the Kurds and Shi'ites, who make up four-fifths of the population of that country. "Were U.S. troops to leave Iraq today, the Baathists, the military, and the tribal leaders would likely join forces to exterminate AQI in short order." Anthony Cordesman, a security analyst at the Center for Strategic and International Studies, agrees: "If we withdraw from Iraq, a lot of the tensions we see today are going to be directed against al-Qaeda as well as against every other faction. So it's not going to be some sort of easy sanctuary for al-Qaeda."[4] Furthermore, says *Time* magazine reporter Michael Duffy, the Anbar Salvation Council "has been aggressively targeting al-Qaeda in that province, denying it safe haven in places it once controlled with an iron fist."[5]

2) The neocons argue that if the U.S. leaves Iraq, the Sunni-Shi'ite civil war would escalate out of control and likely cause regional war as Iraq's neighbors step into the fray. But, says Dreyfus, "the civil war is limited by physical constraints. Neither the Sunnis nor the Shiites have much in the way of armor or heavy weapons." Additionally, since the U.S. trains and arms the Shiites, they are inflaming the war far more than other nations would, since neither Shiite Iran nor Sunni Arab countries would likely risk a regional war by bringing heavy weapons to their counterparts in Iraq.

Dreyfus makes an observation which is all-too-often ignored: "Historically, the vast majorities of Iraqis have not primarily identified themselves according to their sect, as Sunnis or Shiites. Of course, as the civil war escalates, more Iraqis are identifying by sects, and tensions are worsening."

This raises the question as to whether petitioning Iraq was or is the best solution. Chaim Kaufmann, Associate Professor of International Relations at Lehigh University, argues that the international community has learned from our experience in Bosnia that "when a war passes its tipping point—when a critical mass of people is so frightened for its safety that it is no longer possible for any authority in either ethnic group to stop their own community's death squads—

the process of ethnic separation becomes nearly impossible to prevent." In the last chapter, we examined the process the Pentagon has engaged in in training Iraqi death squads, and that was in 2005. Now, Kaufmann argues, "the war has passed its tipping point. The people of central Iraq so concerned with their family's physical safety that it is impossible for any authority, in either the Sunni or Shia communities, to restrain the ethnic cleansers and sectarian militants within their own groups."[6] Thus, partitioning Iraq is inevitable. The arguments about it are moot, if Kaufmann is reasoning correctly. It appears he is.

Partitioning, however, will continue to be a bloody mess. So what is the best role for the U.S. in the mess in Iraq? We begin our analysis with an obvious comment: U.S. withdrawal is not a sufficient condition for insurgent attacks to stop. However, it may be a necessary condition for the end of the insurgency. The problem is, as we have seen, that the "terrorists" who comprise the insurgency are responding to the continued presence of U.S. troops there. So redeploying those troops would certainly be a necessary condition for the attacks to stop. However, if we allowed the international community to replace U.S. forces and focus on rebuilding the infrastructure of Iraq, with significant financial commitments to doing so, Iraq could settle into a peaceful, and possibly prodemocratic, nation. The chances of the U.S. doing that are slim, however, for the reasons given above: we have been on a path to oil control and regional dominance for many years. It would take a decided shift in U.S. foreign policy and domestic philosophy for that to happen. For example, a significant investment in alternative energy sources, such as renewal energy, would alleviate the problem of oil in short order. But as Chalmers Johnson argues so eloquently, America must now make a choice: democracy at home or empire abroad. We can no longer afford to do both, either economically or politically.[7] If we choose democracy, withdrawal from Iraq is essential, and we had better be prepared for a refocused United States as (perhaps) a first among equals, and we had better begin to develop alternatives to oil energy.

As idealistic as this proposal sounds, it is the other side of the historical U.S. interests in the region. If these interests do not change, the quest for empire will continue to push forward regardless of the cost, economically, militarily, or with our domestic life, and we would ultimately face economic weakness and political defeat of democracy at home. The choice seems to be an exclusive disjunction: withdraw or do not withdraw. There are consequences to either choice, and the dilemma is that the consequences of each disjunct are costly and require long-term commitment and significant economic support. The question becomes which option is less costly, better for America, and moral all at the same time. It would seem that, given the expense of lives, morals, and money so far spent in Iraq, with no end in sight, withdrawal and refocus is the better of the two options, both morally and economically.

Summary of our Examination

We have seen in this examination of the decision to invade Iraq that there are at least four converging factors that led to the invasion: the general philosophy of Realpolitik of the U.S. government, which is used to support Mid East and Central American dominance; critical thinking lapses and information ignorance on the part of the media, translated to the populace, particularly concerning the public debate on invading Iraq; violations of basic ethical principles; violations of international law.

Generally, the philosophical reasons our government led us down this path to invasion stem from three things we have examined:
- the history of U.S. ambitions in the Middle East;
- imperialist philosophy of the U.S. government;
- neocon philosophy of Leo Strauss and his followers.

Specifically, there were numerous critical thinking mistakes made in the public debate over going to war on Iraq that we have seen in this study. Just by way of example, here are a few of the critical thinking lapses we have seen in this study:
- *A lack of evidence* for justifying the invasion, especially in Colin Powell's speech to the United Nations.
- *Hasty Generalizations*—i.e. drawing the strongest possible conclusions from weak evidence for the conclusions.
- *Suppressed Evidence*—i.e. picking only evidence that supported the predetermined U.S. administration conclusion that an invasion of Iraq was needed. This includes redefining terms to better suit their position (e.g. "deterrence;" "torture"). It also includes ignoring evidence such as increasing Iraqi compliance with U.N. mandates for inspections and WMD destruction; doubts about the American case for the invasion expressed other U.S. government agencies (e.g. CIA) as well as U.N. inspectors and groups (e.g. IAEA).
- *False Premises*—Facts given were erroneously stated or just plain false, and were shown to be so *at the time* they were being used.
- *Questionable Sources*—e.g. Iraqi defectors (some unnamed; some named), shown *at the time* they were being used to be bogus witnesses with bogus information; rejecting reports from other government agencies (e.g. CIA) in favor in insider administration reports (e.g. Douglas Feith).
- *Arguments from Ignorance*—e.g. Iraq did not prove that they did not possess WMD's, so they are hiding something and/or they must have them.
- *Non-sequiturs*—when attempting to compile evidence to meet normative criteria (either ethical or legal), the premises given were in some

cases not necessary and in nearly all cases insufficient to support the conclusion that the invasion of Iraq was justified.
- *Vague and overly-broad generalizations* in premises and conclusions—e.g. Iraq is "a terrorist entity that has attempted to reach beyond its own borders to support and engage in illegal activities" (John Nichols).
- *Characterizations* used in place of evidence—e.g. "Butcher of Baghdad;" "Dr. Death;" "Chemical Ali;" "he has gassed his own people," etc.
- *Use of circumstantial evidence* to justify conclusions—e.g. Christopher Hitchens argued that Saddam Hussein "harbors every species of gangster" but presented only one very dubious case (al Zarqawi).
- *Red Herring/Post hoc fallacies*—e.g. "humanitarian intervention" in 2003 as necessary, but such arguments were based on pre-1991 actions done by Hussein. In addition, the same arguments ignored the fact that U.S. sanctions and regular missile attacks on Iraq both caused and deepened the humanitarian crisis in Iraq.
- *Contradictions*—e.g. U.S. does not have to follow the U.N., but the U.S. is fulfilling U.N. resolutions in invading Iraq.
- *Failure to take proper accounting of potential consequences* from the invasion and occupation of Iraq.

There were also numerous ethical violations in the public case for going to war that we have examined in this book:
- *Use of self-interest over principle*—the latter is engaged with general or universal rules of conduct toward others.
- *Ignoring or flatly rejecting international law*—e.g. Nuremberg Charter; Geneva Conventions; U.N. Charter, etc.
- *Moral inconsistency*—i.e. picking and choosing which U.N. resolutions to follow, and also using principles to support self-interest.
- *Interpreting U.N. resolutions* narrowly or broadly to suit the U.S. interest in invading Iraq.
- *Hubris*—believing that conquering Iraq would be quick and easy (a "cakewalk" according to Assistant Defense Secretary Ken Adelman), and that we would be "greeted as liberators" (Vice President Cheney), and that, while the rest of the world disputed the U.S. concerning the morality of an invasion, the U.S., with its presumed exceptionalism, believed it had the moral and/or legal right to unilaterally invade anyway (with only a bit of assistance from a few other countries).
- *Ignoring or giving only superficial acknowledgement* of the rigorous requirements of Just War Theory.
- *Refusal to negotiate with Iraq or cooperate with the United Nations*—both are requirements of Just War Theory, but also related to hubris.
- *Preventive war* (as distinguished from pre-emptive war).

- *Piling on the bad behaviors of Saddam Hussein* as premises for invasion, without listing or naming the distinctly moral premises needed to conclude from those bad behaviors that an invasion was justified.
- *Double standards regarding U.S. actions and Iraqi alleged actions*—e.g. support of terrorists, as in Luis Posada Carilles living with impunity in Miami, and Iraq allegedly harboring al Zarqawi.
- *Duplicity* (Machiavellianism)—appealing to high-sounding norms (e.g. freedom; liberation; democracy) while engaging in precisely the opposite behavior (e.g. invasion; domination; control; ethnic cleansing; targeting civilians and infrastructure; torture).
- *Disrespect for the national sovereignty and territorial integrity of Iraq.*
- *Violation of Iraqi civilians*—between 500,000 and one million Iraqi citizens are dead either through or as a consequence of the U.S. invasion.
- *Damage to America's reputation and economy.*
- *American military casualties and the wrecked lives* of the thousands of American families whose loved ones have been (and will be) killed in Iraq.
- *Torture.*

Given all this, it is legitimate and proper to ask whether or not the Iraq debate in the U.S. was done incompetently (as indicated above) or deceptively (as the title of this text indicates). The answer, based on this study is: "both." We have highlighted some of the logical and ethical incompetence of the main public debaters on the invasion, and we have shown some of the obvious duplicity involved and known at the time to be duplicitous. This is arguably what shamed Colin Powell from public life, as he said that it was a permanent blot on his record.[8]

But for more specific evidence of duplicity, one might turn to a good study of the Iraq invasion debate by the group Public Integrity. In a study entitled "False Pretenses," they document 935 lies about Iraq told by the Bush administration—President George Bush, Vice President Dick Cheney, Secretary of State Colin Powell, National Security Advisor Condoleeza Rice, Defense Secretary Donald Rumsfeld, Deputy Defense Secretary Paul Wolfowitz, and White House press secretaries Ari Fleischer and Scott McClellan.[9] The Public Integrity study includes direct quotes, the specific days and occasions on which they were spoken, the evidence existent *at that time* as well as afterwards by which anyone who was watching closely could determine the deceit involved, and video evidence to support the quotations.[10] The lies involved in this study include the Iraq-al Qaeda connection, Iraq's alleged use of aluminum tubes to enrich uranium, Iraq's alleged possession of WMD, Iraq's alleged attempt to purchase "significant quantities of uranium from Africa,"[11] Colin Powell's appeal to "human sources" to present the "facts" about Iraq, and administration claims after the invasion took place that the U.S. found the WMD in two trailers. All of these statements were known by those who were following the issue to be lies at the time they were stated, yet there was little investigation into them, and little tolerance for dissent from these official pronouncements. This leads to the next issue.

First Steps: What Must We Do to Avoid this Deception in the Future?

First, we citizens must become—and remain—more informed about the workings of our government and what they are doing than we have heretofore been. Granting from the start that there is much that is kept secret from us, the fact of the matter, as has been demonstrated in this book, is that enough information was available to us prior to the invasion of Iraq on March 19, 2003, to cogently debate the issue and to come to the conclusion that such a proposal was unfounded empirically, not logically sound, unethical in its formulation, and illegal according to international law. These are all categories of knowledge which citizens must be as adept at engaging as they can be. That is the only way to stop this type of action from happening again.

Second, we, the citizens of the United States, must return to distinctively ethical principles and values rather than purely pragmatic dialogue and actions. This must be accompanied by a development of critical thinking when it comes to government pronouncements and propaganda intended to take us to war. We must demand of government accountability, and that implies that we become informed of the issues at hand.

With the bulk of the prominent pre-war support of the U.S. invasion of Iraq focused on Utilitarian/pragmatic method and most of the arguments opposing the invasion grounded in Just War Theory calls to follow international law, it becomes clear that the United States faced a choice before initiating the war on Iraq: it could be a moral state, engaged in mutual international cooperation and support, a "good citizen" of the world community by following international law, or it could set aside its moral principles, follow the path of unilateralism and self-interest as its guiding norms, and thereby lose its status as a moral leader in the world and as a first nation among equals by ignoring the general will of the world. That we chose the latter course is more the pity, the consequences of which we have yet to see.

Third, we must demand more from our media. The media, from the ostensibly liberal *New York Times* to FOX News, was not only completely delinquent in actually investigating the government case for invading Iraq, but they in fact served as volunteer cheerleaders for the invasion. Judith Miller at the *Times* was responsible for pushing the now-famous "Iraq aluminum tubes" lie, and for reporting, on the basis of second-hand sources, that the U.S. had found the Iraqi WMD's they were looking for. Katie Couric gushed as the anchor of NBC's *Today* program that "I think Navy SEALs rock!"[12] and Dan Rather pandered that "I want my country to win, whatever the definition of 'win' may be. Now, I can't and don't argue that that is coverage without prejudice." The American media has been nothing short of disgraceful in its coverage of the planned Iraq invasion.[13] Even worse, this media, with few exceptions, has shown its willingness to capitulate its duty to inform citizens and to challenge those in power, in favor of obliging the interests of those in power, to the point that one might rightfully ask what the difference is between American media and former Soviet-owned media.

This is not new: the same pattern has replayed throughout U.S. history. The government lies, the U.S. corporatized media uncritically and complicitly replays the lie and even magnifies it by advocating its support, in the face of evidence to the contrary, the war is commenced, the truth starts to overtake the lies, people withdraw their support, the war drags on. We have seen this pattern repeatedly in American history: USS Maine (1898); Gulf of Tonkin (1964); Dominican Republic (1965); Grenada (1983); Panama (1989); Kosovo (1999); Iraq (2002-2003), just to name a few of the more prominent cases.[14] The case of media complicity in the planned Iraq invasion is demonstrated clearly by the overwhelming voice given to pro-war advocates and the marginalization of dissenting voices. In one study, conducted by Fairness and Accuracy in Reporting, the following media outlets were studied: ABC World News Tonight, CBS Evening News, NBC Nightly News, and PBS NewsHour with Jim Lehrer. The study lasted about two weeks, from 1/30/03-2/12/03.[15] A total of 393 on-camera sources were on these programs, more than two-thirds of whom were U.S. citizens, and more than 75% of whom were former military officials. Only three of the 393 sources used were anti-war, less than 1%. If media-maintained government propaganda trumping up war support is nothing new, then pre-Iraq invasion coverage fit right in with our history. We need news sources for democracy to function properly as invoking an open dialogue, not as Stalin-like propaganda machines for government manipulation of the populace by extreme one-sidedness. This is why it is critically important that citizens become more sophisticated about what they consume as truth. This implies using several sources of information, and that we avoid relying heavily on what is euphemistically called the "mainstream media."

Fourth, we must demand that our government follow international law. If anything should convince us of the need for the adherence of all nations to international law and its standards, it is the shift of the United States from a nation which at least acknowledged the rule of law to the rogue state that we have become in foreign affairs through the policies of the Bush administration. This is particularly true with regard to our invasion and occupation of Iraq. Condemned by international law and the world at large, it is a glaring instance of the need for compliance with international law on the part of all nations.

Why is international law so important?

First of all, international law is a critical part of and the legal and institutional expression of our deepest moral thoughts and principles. When it comes to questions of war, it is part of what Michael Walzer calls "the war convention." Walzer assumes its legitimacy, as well he should. But the U.S. does not. Without it though, the moral fabric that structures international relations would be irreparably damaged, as the structures of states' actions and discourse will have broken down. No progress in morality or even civilization is possible without rules of social discourse and engagement. We may extend the argument given by the German philosopher Jurgen Habermas regarding constitutional democracies. Habermas argues that the condition for democracy is what he calls "the Discourse Principle:" "Only those norms are valid to which all affected persons could agree as participants in rational discourses."[16] Thus, the system of rights in society consists in precisely the fact that it states the conditions under which "the forms of communication necessary for the genesis of legitimate law can be legally institutionalized."[17] Although Habermas specifically says he is uninterested in using his theory to justify international law, there is no reason we cannot extend it to this realm.[18] Habermas himself opens the door for that.[19] Since this is beyond the pale of our concerns here, I simply want to suggest that international law is an integral part of peaceful cooperation between persons in the world, if not between nations. It spells out the conditions under which we might thrive in a world community.

Second, dismantling or ignoring international law for the sake of one nation's interests, as the U.S. has a history of doing, especially noticeable in the George W. Bush administration, makes nuclear war inevitable. The reason for this is that there would be no controlling mechanism to stop the proliferation or use of such weapons. Michael McGwire, a prominent strategic analyst, states it forthrightly: the success of the effort "to eliminate the threat of global nuclear war" depends upon the effectiveness of international agreements such as the Nuclear Proliferation Treaty.[20] The United States has taken the lead among nuclear nations in *not* following the NPT. In 1996, the World Court unanimously ruled that the nuclear powers are legally obligated to bring nuclear disarmament under control by negotiations. Yet the Bush administration has been the only country in the world to flatly reject the World Court ruling and the NPT by increasing our nuclear weapons programs and stipulating the right of the U.S. to a first nuclear strike.

Third, terrorism becomes inevitable as a response to powerful nations exercising their own will in the world with impunity. Historically, it is always the case that oppressed peoples seek ways of exploiting the vulnerability of their oppressors. The experience of England with India in the early twentieth century attests to this, as does the experience of the United States in Iraq and elsewhere. Terrorism itself is really a response to oppression, and when it is directed our way, it is a response to Western imperialism. It will continue as long as we continue to be a rogue state (i.e. a state which eschews international laws and standards).

Fourth, no international cooperation is possible without international law. Nations need structure in order to work together, and international law is that structure. McGwire again writes that the most important reason to condemn the invasion of Iraq was that "such an operation threatened to undermine the very fabric of international relations. That decision repudiated a century of slow, intermittent and often painful progress toward an international system based on cooperative security . . . agreed norms of behaviour and a steadily growing fabric of law."[21]

The importance of international law is underscored when we realize that there is no true security between nations without it. How can one nation condemn another for its actions if there is no ground for condemnation?

Furthermore, we can easily craft a parallel example of the need of all nations, including the United States, to acknowledge and follow international law. Think about the chaos that would result in society if there was no law in personal or communal life. Or to make this analogy closer to our current situation in the world today, what would happen if the elites—those with power and wealth inside our country—were permitted to violate every law and create their own, while the rest of us were forced to adhere to whatever laws they chose for us, all the while knowing their lawlessness? Would this not be a sufficient condition for social chaos, violence, and rebellion against them?

In addition to all this, there can be no real society and certainly no world order or even true peace, without international law. Philosophers and judges throughout history have been nearly unanimously made this claim. They cannot be detailed here, but the defenses of the need for law in relations within society and between nations come from thinkers as diverse as Thomas Hobbes, John Locke, John Rawls, and Noam Chomsky. But perhaps foreign policy scholar Michael MccGwire put it best, as he presented his reasoning why the decision to invade Iraq was a dangerous and terribly misguided one:

> That decision repudiated a century of slow, intermittent and often painful progress toward an international system based on cooperative security...agreed norms of behaviour and a steadily growing fabric of law[22]

More important that this, all principles of ethical conduct and thus law are based on the principle of universality: "If one does it, then anyone may do it." Think of what would happen if every nation in the world made the same claims that the U.S. has done, does now, and did with abandon under the Bush administration regarding invasion of other countries and the right to nuclear first strikes.

Furthermore, without rule of law, no criticism of other nations is possible. How could the United States criticize Iraqi non-compliance with U.N. resolutions when the Bush team stated repeatedly that the U.S. did not have to abide by U.N. resolutions, in many cases the very same resolutions to which Bush was holding Iraq? The contradiction is laughable, but no one is laughing about it in Iraq today.

For these and many other reasons, it is time for us to focus on requiring our leaders to follow international law and to become world citizens again instead of the rogue and self-centered nation that appears to be the basis of the Bush administration foreign policy.

The Starting Point for the Next Version of the U.S. War on Terrorism: How Does One War On a (Vague) Concept?

Everyone seems to know terrorism when they see it, but no one seems to be able to define it. Such is the fate of philosophers who attempt to tackle this thorny issue. What is terrorism? It is a question which still echoes through discourses, articles, and debates, academic and otherwise. In this section, we will attempt to provide a general definition of terrorism that hopefully would satisfy all parties to the debate. From there we will discuss whether Just War criteria permits the war of a state with a non-governmental group we call "terrorists," and conclude with a discussion concerning whether or not terrorism is ever morally justifiable.

As a way of underscoring the importance of this need for clear definitions in the alleged "war on terrorism," it would assist us to review our history to see how often the United States has declared war on terrorism. A brief review will suffice to make this point.

The Reagan administration, upon taking office in 1981, declared a U.S. "war on terror" in Nicaragua, El Salvador, and Guatemala. It also declared the war on terror against Muammar Qaddafi's Libya. It extended the war on terrorism into the drug trade, which was said to finance those who would overthrow American democracy. This latter declaration ended with a new President, George H.W. Bush, invading Panama, retaking the Canal, and arresting and extraditing Panamanian President Manuel Noriega on drug trafficking charges. When George W. Bush took office, filling his cabinet with Reagan and Bush I leftovers, it should have come as no surprise that he declared a "war on terror" once again, after 9/11, and this time targeted North Korea, Syria, Iraq, Afghanistan, and Iran. It worked in the 1980's, so why not in the 2000's? The same strategy works for U.S.-backed governments such as Israel: declare a war on terrorism, and then do what you will, militarily, all the while appealing to self-defense under Article 51 of the U.N. Charter.[23]

The problem that immediately besets us is seen in the title to this section. Are we warring on terror—i.e. a tactic; a verb—or are we warring on terrorists, non-state individuals and/or groups? If we cannot define who or what we are warring against, we cannot meet the ethical and legal requirements regarding, for example, proper intention and discrimination. This is especially true when terrorism is defined only in the context of non-state actors. Legitimate questions may then be raised concerning how the principles and the laws of war are to be applied, or indeed, if they can really be applied at all. These significant questions are beyond our purview here. Suffice it to say that discussing the definition of this "war on terrorism" is critical for the actions in which we as a country are now said to be engaged.

The definitions that we will review seem to indicate that the war is on a tactic. But perhaps we need to define the tactic in order to know who it is we are warring against. It is this problem, and the problem of agreeing upon a definition to begin with, that makes this new kind of war so perplexing and vague. It will make for formidable problems in cleanly applying the traditional Just War Theory to it.

The definition of terrorism is complex and varied. Philosophers debate among themselves whether it is a necessary condition for the definition of terrorism that it includes attacks on civilians, and/or attacks on revered objects or the environment.

Since the United States government is currently fighting the latest version of the "war on terrorism," we would do best to begin with the definition they give of "terrorism." Although the U.S. has several different definitions of this term, depending on which department of the government one looks, there are common elements to each one. The Defense Department defines terrorism as "the calculated use of unlawful violence or threat of unlawful violence to inculcate fear; intended to coerce or to intimidate governments or societies in the pursuit of goals that are generally political, religious, or ideological."[24] The FBI stipulates that "terrorism is the unlawful use of force and violence against persons or property to intimidate or coerce a government, the civilian population, or any segment thereof, in furtherance of political or social objectives,"[25] while the State Department defines terrorism to be "premeditated politically-motivated violence perpetrated against non-combatant targets by sub-national groups or clandestine agents, usually intended to influence an audience."[26] The official U.S. Code divides terrorism into two kinds, hence, two definitions. According to Title 18, Part I, Chapter 113B, "international terrorism" means activities that:

(A) involve violent acts or acts dangerous to human life that are a violation of the criminal laws of the United States or of any State, or that would be a criminal violation if committed within the jurisdiction of the United States or of any State;

(B) appear to be intended—
    (i) to intimidate or coerce a civilian population;
    (ii) to influence the policy of a government by intimidation or coercion; or
    (iii) to affect the conduct of a government by mass destruction, assassination, or kidnapping; and

(C) occur primarily outside the territorial jurisdiction of the United States, or transcend national boundaries in terms of the means by which they are accomplished, the persons they appear intended to intimidate or coerce, or the locale in which their perpetrators operate or seek asylum;

"Domestic terrorism" means activities that—

(A) involve acts dangerous to human life that are a violation of the criminal laws of the United States or of any State;

(B) appear to be intended—
    (i) to intimidate or coerce a civilian population;
    (ii) to influence the policy of a government by intimidation or coercion; or

(iii) to affect the conduct of a government by mass destruction, assassination, or kidnapping; and

(C) occur primarily within the territorial jurisdiction of the United States.

In the U.S. definition of terrorism then, the key elements are unlawful violence, fear/intimidation, targeted at civilians, for political ends and for the final end of influencing "an audience." That audience, presumably, is the U.S. government itself, but it could also be the populace who is attacked. In fact, the British and the United Nations hold similar definitions with similar key elements, even though they differ a bit in their expression. The U.N. does not have an official definition of terrorism, but it does maintain an "academic consensus" definition. In this definition, it adds "anxiety-inspiring" and "repeated" to the constitutive elements of their definition:

"Terrorism is an anxiety-inspiring method of repeated violent action, employed by (semi-) clandestine individual, group or state actors, for idiosyncratic, criminal or political reasons, whereby—in contrast to assassination—the direct targets of violence are not the main targets. The immediate human victims of violence are generally chosen randomly (targets of opportunity) or selectively (representative or symbolic targets) from a target population, and serve as message generators. Threat- and violence-based communication processes between terrorist (organization), (imperiled) victims, and main targets are used to manipulate the main target (audience(s)), turning it into a target of terror, a target of demands, or a target of attention, depending on whether intimidation, coercion, or propaganda is primarily sought."[27]

We encounter immediate problems with such definitions. Are the actions of a state which fit these descriptions while fighting terrorism themselves terrorist? If so, then there are a plethora of actions of the United States that could rightfully be considered to be terrorism, such as the support of the Contras in Nicaragua, the attacks on Grenada and Panama, and both wars on Iraq. Alison Jaggar makes an even more critical point: the U.S. definition rules out any possibility of state terrorism.[28] As Chomsky notes, the definitions make no distinction between terrorism and counterterrorism, the latter of which is official U.S. policy. Nor do the definitions distinguish between international terrorism and aggression, nor between terrorism and resistance (e.g. freedom fighters).[29] Were Nelson Mandela and the African National Congress terrorists or freedom fighters? The U.S. and Israel were the sole nations to hold to the former, as evidenced by their vote on the 1987 U.N. General Assembly resolution that recognized "the right to self-determination, freedom, and independence" of people "forcibly deprived" by "colonial and racist regimes and foreign occupations," and that these very rights, placed in a proclamation condemning terrorism, were to be held as prior in importance to the characterization of those who sought them as terrorists.[30] The vote was 153-2, the U.S. and Israel casting the only no votes.

Can philosophers aid in making the critical distinctions about terrorism that will allow us to come to a clearer understanding of what it is? If we do not have a clear definition, moral analysis will be difficult if not impossible. So our first task has been set for us: is there a definition of terrorism that makes the necessary distinctions that enable us to make a clearer analysis of violent actions?

The definition of terrorism provided by Michael Walzer is spread out through the first part of his chapter on terrorism (Chapter 12) in *Just and Unjust Wars*. The first part of his definition concerns its method and goal:

> Its purpose is to destroy the morale of a nation or a class, to undercut its solidarity; its method is the random murder of innocent people. Randomness is the crucial feature of terrorist activity.[31]

If it is true that the operative element of terrorism is its random targeting, that is, that it targets innocents, isn't much of the bombing that is done in a conventional (justified) war also terrorism, rather than simply a violation of *jus in bello* criteria? For example, is not the attack on Fallujah a perfect fit for Walzer's definition of terrorism? It would seem so. It was "the random murder of innocent people."[32] So how does Walzer propose to distinguish terrorism from justified acts of war? It seems to be in the concept of "targeting," but if this is true, then the bombings of Dresden, Hiroshima, Nagasaki, and Fallujah, among others, are all cases of terrorism. However, Walzer denies this. He actually supports the bombings in the first three cases on the grounds of state "Supreme Emergency," defined as the nature and imminence of a danger to the state (i.e. how close the danger is and how serious it is), that allows it to break the war convention.[33] In brief, the doctrine of supreme emergency allows a state to kill innocent civilians (e.g. over 300,000 in Walzer's example of legitimate supreme emergency in the bombing of German cities), whereas no reason is permitted for "terrorists" to make any similar claim to killing innocents.

That Walzer denies to "terrorists" the moral leverage to kill civilians that he allows to the state—even though for different reasons for each—demonstrates a significant inconsistency in his examination of terrorism. Thus, we must examine this argument.

Walzer states that the reason "terrorists" claim to kill innocents is that of "military necessity," defined by the claim that "there no alternative to terrorist activity if oppressed peoples are to be liberated."[34] Further, Walzer claims that it is said by terrorists that it is their only means to liberation. The reason that Walzer denies this claim to terrorists is that it explodes all moral limits in violence:

> It shatters the war convention and the political code. It breaks across moral limits beyond which no further limitation seems possible, for within the categories of civilian and citizen, there isn't any smaller group for which immunity might be claimed.[35]

The "terrorist" appeal to military necessity is specifically that an attack "is necessary to compel enemy submission with the least expenditure of time, life, and money."[36] But, says Walzer, no such "terrorist" attack in history can make this claim.[37] Those that do, "erase all moral distinctions along with the men and women who painfully worked them out."[38]

On the other hand, the state is permitted to kill civilians, and in far larger numbers than "terrorists" do, all for the sake of supreme emergency; that is, a nation that is faced with defeat by what may be considered a far greater evil (e.g. Hitler). For Walzer, "a world where entire peoples are enslaved or massacred is literally unbearable," because "the survival and freedom of political communities...are the highest values of international society."[39] Further, such a supreme emergency can be directed against a single nation (e.g. Hitler's Germany). Thus, a state under such threat may respond by killing civilians and breaking that nation's morale[40]—i.e. state terrorism.

What are we to make of this argument? First, by denying to terrorists what he permits to the state—even though each entity ostensibly supports its actions by different reasons—Walzer demonstrates both a conceptual and a moral inconsistency. First, such a tactic ends up privileging the state over freedom fighters or "terrorists" regarding who may kill whom. Threats to the existence of the state by those whom the state deems to be a great evil may be met with extreme violence, yet those whom the state threatens are prohibited from such violence. Remember that he classifies terrorists as groups that "kill anybody."[41] But now state terrorism is permitted because it is the state's—i.e. the state can make the call between waging "a determinate crime (the killing of innocent people)" and an "immeasurable evil (a Nazi triumph)."[42] But to quote Walzer from his argument condemning political assassination, this issue is a judgment call.[43] In the case of the state, it is a legitimate one; in the case of the terrorist, not. Historical examples aside, there is a conceptual and moral inconsistency in permitting one group to commit the horrendous acts denied to the other group. It cannot be simply that the reasons of one group do not match historical events so far while those of the other group do, as Walzer claims, for it is logically conceivable that the judgment call of terrorists (e.g. in Afghanistan and Iraq) is that of an immeasurable evil (e.g. U.S. brutal occupation of each country, its partitioning the country in the case of Iraq in order to break it up, such that the nation no longer effectively exists, and certainly not as the unity it had been. Walzer defends killing civilians in this instance, as we have seen. When one adds to this the imposition of American capitalism, individualism, and from the Mid East point of view, licentiousness and even lawlessness, it is easily seen as the direct, immediate, and deeply dangerous threat to not only their nation, but to their sedentary cultural mores). How is one to logically or morally discount one judgment of the dangerous and proximate evil that allows for the "supreme emergency" legitimating killing civilians, yet discount the other judgment that military necessity allows attacks on civilians? The difference, for Walzer, is in the claim of terrorism to military necessity; only a state may have the supreme emergency just described. Yet, if the danger is real, dangerous, and coming with overwhelming force and power ("shock and awe") to a people or culture that is clearly outmanned by this evil, why is there nothing similar allowed for them? This leads to the second issue: that moral principles must apply equally if they are to be called moral at all, especially in cases in which one is drawing moral boundaries around potential target groups like civilians. While Walzer acknowledges this, he still gives precedence to the "necessary evil" that the state may commit against innocents, which he says is unnecessary in the case of terrorist attacks. It would seem, then, that the existence of the state is worth preserving over the liberation of a people from oppression.

Notice that terrorism has liberation of a people as its goal, even in Walzer's definition of its claim to military necessity. How does Walzer's denial of the right of such "terrorists" to kill civilians square with United Nations Resolution 42, which grants to liberation groups the right to fight for "the inalienable right to self-determination and independence"? If the state has a right to preserve its existence against extreme evil by killing civilians directly in the process, and national liberation movements are legitimated by international law, why are they not permitted the same right in Walzer's theory? The evil of oppression involved in each scenario is the same.

Further, what does one do with a group struggling against the occupation of a foreign army, or a case of a totalitarian regime? If that group attacks the single class of politicians who are responsible for such oppression, they are labeled as terrorist according to Walzer's definition. But would this classification not justify state oppression and also the occupation of other countries on the grounds that the freedom fighters would have no alternative but to directly oppose an army whose strength far exceeds it? Walzer calls terrorism a "way of avoiding engagement with the enemy army." In addition, he notes that the war convention and international law puts political leaders into the class of people who are immune from attack. Does this not he put the freedom fighters in the impossible position of either fighting directly against the oppressor's army only—a war which they would surely lose—or choose the route of pacifism or surrender to domination by superior forces? As he says, "political assassins are simply murderers."[44]

Still, the protection of politicians under the charge of terrorism is a significant problem for Walzer's definition, again because it provides too much preference to the state and severely limits legitimate struggles against totalitarian and/or occupying states. Nor does Walzer include the notion of "threat to use violence" for his stated terrorist ends; something that ought to be examined as well.

Walzer responds to this putative allegation with two conceptions. First, he stipulates that, on the assumption that a regime is in fact oppressive, "one should look for agents of oppression and not simply for government agents."[45] However, he almost immediately adds an exception. In some cases, he states, "'just assassinations' are at least possible," if those who do it renounce "every other kind" of killing may be "marked off from those who kill at random."[46] So, political assassinations, *sans* the targeting of civilians, are not always cases of terrorism. But terrorism, he says, kills ordinary citizens. "The names and occupations of the dead are not known in advance."[47]

Second, it is because "terrorists kill anybody" they cannot appeal to what he calls military necessity, because of their indiscriminate killing.[48] This means, for Walzer, that for them "anything goes" in war. All moral constraints are removed and war becomes total if terrorism, defined as randomly killing civilians (including politicians, in most cases), is permitted and justified under any circumstances. This move to total war that terrorism embraces is what concerns Walzer the most. Again, though, this still does not fully address the issue of freedom fighters, since the definition is not one of necessarily targeting civilians. One would think that, given his defense of political assassinations, Walzer would uphold freedom fighting of an oppressor as well, provided it does not target civilians.

As a final observation, notice how Walzer shifts in his moral methodology, from deontological principle to utilitarian calculation of proportionality. Whereas his appeal has consistently been to the war convention, international law, and Just War Theory to condemn terrorism, when it comes to *state* terrorism, now called "supreme emergency," the appeal shifts to the proportional assessment involved in calculating dead civilians versus defeat of a nation by a great evil. While Walzer acknowledges the shift, he limits it by stating that "it is the acknowledgement of rights that puts a stop to such [utilitarian] calculations."[49] Thus, his ultimate appeal is to the "destruction of the innocent," which, "whatever its purposes, is a kind of blasphemy against our deepest moral convictions."[50] Is it this "blasphemy" that he finds lacking in "terrorism"?

Shannon E. French tends to agree with Walzer, holding terrorism to be murder, not warrior-like in its action. It is interesting to note that the very description French makes places a moral judgment on it; that is, terrorism necessarily attacks noncombatants and that is necessary immoral, while the noble warrior does not do that.[51] But much more problematic for French's understanding of terrorism (she does not take pains to define it in her article), is that she assumes a number of things. First, that terrorism *necessarily* directly and intentionally targets noncombatants. The dubious nature of that assumption is something we shall examine below. Second, her understanding raises another question, not dealt with in her article: is it ever permissible to target noncombatants and not be terrorists? French would say no, but Michael Walzer says yes, and he presents the example of the British nighttime indiscriminate bombing of German cities early in the war. Because Britain had "no other way" to stop a Nazi victory, their bombing was justified.[52] If Walzer is correct, Shannon's analysis is incorrect. However, they do share the same understanding of terrorism, and that is that terrorists *necessarily* target innocents. Finally, for French's analysis, violations of the discrimination principle of Just War Theory would have to be classified as murder.[53] But if indiscriminate soldiers are murderers, and terrorists are murderers, and both are such because they directly target innocents, then what is the difference between their actions? We are, as French says, back to the criterion of just cause, perhaps. But if just cause distinguishes murder from terrorism, it is a weak foundation, because terrorists might well have just cause on their side, as we shall see below.

For both Walzer and French, the definition of a terrorist has on overt and unapologetic moral condemnation built into it. That strikes me as a question-begging definition. When one defines terrorism as an immoral act, one not only overlooks other salient features of terrorism, but one has already performed a moral analysis in the very act of defining it. What would be more interesting and helpful is if we defined terrorism in a nonjudgmental way and then performed a moral analysis. That is what I seek to do here.

There are nearly as many definition of terrorism as there are writers on it.[54] However, the one thing that most of them seem to have in common is that terrorist attacks necessarily target civilians. We will thus confine our remarks to two areas of concern: the targeting of civilians as a necessary condition of the definition of terrorism, and the attempts of writers like Walzer and French to define terrorism morally.[55]

Virginia Held rejects the definitions of both Walzer and by implication French, that terrorism is necessarily aimed at civilians. Specifically, those definitions are too constricted because terrorists do not attack only "innocent people." This can be seen in the examples of the attack on the marine barracks in Beirut in 1983 and the USS Cole bombing in 2000. In both cases the casualties were military, but the commonly accepted understanding of terrorism called both actions "terrorist." Thus, Held offers what she considers to be a more acceptable definition: "political violence that usually involves sudden attacks to spread fear to a wider group than those attacked, often doing so by attacking civilians."[56]

She also takes sharp issue with the definition Walzer presents for several reasons. First, his definition would have to separate the attacks on the World Trade Center from the attacks on the Pentagon on 9/11/01, and call the first attack terrorist, but not the second. This seems strained. Second, using civilians as a necessary condition for the definition places the burden of "being a 'legitimate target' on the lowest levels of the military hierarchy . . . and exempts the persons who give them their orders."[57] Third, there is no clear distinction between noncombatants and legitimate targets in Walzer's criteria. For example, "many members of the armed forces are conscripts who have no choice but to be combatants . . . Many other combatants around the world are children." It is also not clear to Held, as it is not to me, that citizens should automatically be exempt from attack if they have demanded of their leaders the use of political violence against another group.

The definition of terrorism provided by Held does help alleviate some of the problems we have seen in Walzer's definition, in that it does not make attacks on civilians a necessary condition, nor does it exclude *a priori* attacks on politicians. Yet it is still insufficient. Is it a necessary condition that the violence be strictly political? Can it be religious as well? She does admit that both poverty and religion are partial causes of terrorism.[58] So the motive of political purposes is as partial as religion and poverty. Further, is (cultural) authoritarianism a necessary condition of defining it properly, as Walzer claims?[59] Held does not address these issues, but there seem to be elements of these in the common understanding of the term. It is fair to submit that these are all necessary conditions of terrorism, so why were these excluded from her definition?

Furthermore, the statement that terrorism "often" attacks civilians implies, of course, that it does not always do so. Held even states that the attack on the U.S. marines in Beirut in 1983 is a case of terrorism. So we must excise attacks on civilians as a necessary condition of the definition of terrorism. But it is the necessary conditions she sets out to find.

In addition, Held does not consider an element that I would say is a necessary condition of the definition of terrorism, and that is its secrecy. No one knows who, what, or when a terrorist attack will occur, and even after it occurs one often does not know who did it. It would seem that this is necessary to understand in order to have a clear conception of terrorism for the purpose of moral analysis. Perhaps this is what she means by "sudden," but I take that term to mean "by surprise," and the latter understanding only covers part of what is implied by the term "secret."

Perhaps in an attempt to avoid the issues that beset Walzer and Held, Alison Jaggar provides what is arguably one of the clearer notions of terrorism:

> extreme threats or violence designed to intimidate or subjugate governments, groups, or individuals . . . aimed directly or immediately at the bodies or belongings of innocent civilians but these are typically terrorists' secondary targets.[60]

The strengths of her definition are precisely the weaknesses of the others. First, it requires that the targets not be simply civilians, but *innocent* civilians. This leaves the possibility open that politicians who order oppressive military operations to be targeted by the opposition. Synopsizing the definition of innocence put forward by Jeffrie Murphy, Jaggar says that innocence means "being a noncombatant." That immediately raises the question concerning the definition of combatant, to which Jaggar, using Murphy, answers

> combatants include all those engaged in the attempt to destroy you, whatever their place in the chain of command or responsibility; thus, they include not only frontline military personnel but also the civilians who issue orders to those personnel.[61]

Her definition provides a number of distinct advantages and strengths not found in any of the definitions we have considered so far. First, it includes targeting certain objects needed by noncombatants, such as water supplies and power sources, as well as the natural environment. It also allows that states can be terrorist as well as non-state groups, something distinctly missing from Walzer's view. Further, the method of terrorism is irrelevant, in the sense that different people are horrified and frightened by different things:

> Terrorist practices are distinguished from more ordinary threats not because they involve any particular methods of producing fear, but instead because they are intended to create a state of fear that is acute and long-lasting enough to influence future behavior.[62]

Thus, the method used, whether it is suicide bombing, assassinations, sabotage, or hostage-taking, is irrelevant to the definition of terrorism. What counts is who is targeted, and if the target is innocent, it is terrorism.

This seems to be the strongest of the definitions we have seen, if for no other reason than that it does not capitulate to the problems the others do. But there is need for something additional. It is equally the means, not simply the goal of terrorism that distinguishes it from justified warfare. The ends of both military and terrorist engagements in some instances are the same: to influence a people and government to change their minds about an issue or issues, religious, political, or generally ideological. It is the means that makes one of these approaches more morally objectionable than the other, and by that I do not mean simply the attack on civilians or innocents, but the *exclusive use of surreptitious means in targeting* either innocents, their property, the environment, *or military targets*, rather than direct and open confrontation. The surreptitiousness involves the who, what, where, and when of a terrorist attack. It is this secrecy on their part, and uncertainty on the part of innocents, that induces as much terror over time as the attack itself. This may or may not be implied in the definition given by Held, but that is not clear. It is not mentioned at all in Jaggar or in Walzer. I wish to make it explicit here.

Given the various understandings of terrorism covered here, we might now be in a position to craft a more expansive definition of terrorism that takes advantage of the strengths of the definition used by Jaggar, but avoids the weaknesses of the others we have seen. To that end, I would propose the following definition of terrorism, in these component elements, which I hold to be individually necessary and jointly sufficient conditions for defining terrorism:

1) Violent acts or threats thereof;
2) Done either in one act or a series;
3) Performed by state or non-state actors;
4) Usually if not always engaged by using secrecy and surprise;
5) Often shocking or spectacular;
6) Chosen for purposes of media coverage and therefore public consumption and awareness;
7) Producing a negative reaction by the populace;
8) Often targeting innocent civilians or their property (i.e. not necessarily or exclusively—Virginia Held is correct. This is the reason for the next element);
9) Involving entities that either do or do not exist in a situation of declared or engaged war, or have no clear just cause involving a whole people;
10) Usually done as part of a longer campaign (i.e. attacks are often serial);

11) Done for the overall purpose of forcing a government to change a policy or policies.

I take elements 1, 3 through 6, and 11 to be uncontroversial as the literature on terrorism uses or acknowledges these elements and with varying degrees of emphasis. As to point 2, this was stated in response to Joseph Boyle, who holds that terrorist actions usually come in "sets" of actions.[63] But it hardly seems sufficient to say, with Boyle, that terrorism is *necessarily* defined as a serial action, for unless one casts a wide conceptual net, the terrorist attack in Spain in 2004 was not followed by any others directed at the population. Nor were there reports of a plan of a series of attacks on Spain. The position Boyle takes also raises the question of how one determines a proper method by which to classify terrorist acts as "serial." Do they have to be directed at one country? Do they have target civilians or can any target count as a serial terrorist strike?

In this definition these conditions are held as individually necessary and jointly sufficient. Element 7 has been defended by Virginia Held, with whom I agree. What I am adding is element 9, which allows for terrorism to be charged from both within and outside of belligerent acts involving a nation's military forces.

One of the advantages to this more complex definition of terrorism is that it avoids the problems that Walzer and French encounter in limiting terrorism to attacks on noncombatants. It avoids the particular problems Walzer has in his statist presuppositions, which morally allows states to engage in terrorist activities without calling them that. In addition, it stays true to the U.S. and U.N. definitions and to common usage, such as the use of violence, attacks on persons or property, and political ends. The U.S. requirement that it "inculcate fear" has been broadened to include "negative reactions" because fear is not the only emotion associated with terrorist attacks. These elements uphold completely the U.N. understanding of terrorism, and they agree with and elaborate upon Alison Jaggar's definition, which I take to be one of the best so far. It avoids the shortcomings of Boyle's definition by admitting that sometimes terrorists have a just cause, and they do not necessary attack civilians, while agreeing with the strength of Boyle's definition that terrorist attacks often come in waves. It expands Held's definition by adding the notion of secrecy while avoiding the contradiction in her own definition—i.e. that terrorism by definition "spreads fear," then her use of the U.S.S. Cole bombing and the Beirut barracks bombing as examples of terrorism. These did not spread fear among the populace, but disgust and anger.

A clear disadvantage of such a definition is that is quite cumbersome, and would make it difficult to use to properly describe an action as terrorism. But because of the broad implications and connotations of the term "terrorism," we must be as precise as possible in our definition, on the pain of being too verbose.

U.S. Terrorism

No analysis of terrorism would be complete without applying suggested definitions. We will do that now, beginning in our own back yard. Whether one uses the definition of terrorism suggested by the U.S. government, the United Nations, or the one I have suggested (but particularly the for which one I am arguing), the U.S. is guilty of consistent, ongoing, and horrendous acts of terrorism. Centered primarily in the Mid East and Central America, but also including diplomatic nods to Russia against the Chechens, U.S. terrorism is rampant and easily seen, once a definition is understood.[64]

The School of the Americas: Headquartered at Fort Benning, Georgia, this is the training ground for U.S. assassins and rebel leaders for Central America. They have been responsible for hundreds of thousands of civilian deaths in Central American countries, including involvement in the murder of six Jesuit priests, their lay coworker, and her daughter, in 1989. There is even evidence that they were behind the assassination of Archbishop Oscar Romero of El Salvador.[65]

Nicaragua: The U.S.-backed the dictatorship of Somoza, whose National Guard murdered thousands of civilians. In 1986, the World Court ruled against the U.S., judging that it had conducted "unlawful use of force" and "methods of coercion"—i.e. terrorism. The Court ruling ordered the U.S. to pay Nicaragua approximately $17 billion in penalties. The U.N. followed suit, proposing a resolution in response to the Court ruling that all nations obey international law. The U.S. vetoed that resolution. Needless to say, the U.S. ignored the World Court ruling, and the oppression and terrorism against the citizens of Nicaragua by the U.S. continues to this day.[66] As a result of U.S. policies there, an estimated 70% of Nicaraguans live in a state of chronic or extreme hunger.[67]

El Salvador: The U.S. backed terrorist squads to harass the democratically elected government and to keep the people so bathed in their own blood that terror ruled the day in the 1980's.

Guatemala: The U.S., in the 1960's, embarked on a program to subvert and overturn popular democracy in Guatemala. In addition, the U.S. supported a well-known murderous thug in Guatemala, Rioss Montt, to prevent the return of such, under the guise of the "democratization" of the country.[68]

Panama: President H.W. Bush, in 1989, invaded and overthrew its president, Manuel Noriega, who had long been a cooperative CIA pawn, but had become uncooperative in recent years. In the process, the U.S. killed thousands of civilians.

East Timor: between 1975 and 1999, the U.S.-backed Indonesian government slaughtered over 200,000 civilians, and continues to do so, while U.S. weapons poured into the country. President Clinton originally continued this policy, but when the atrocities became too much for the world community, which put great pressure on Clinton, he finally withdrew his support for Indonesia, and they withdrew from East Timor as a consequence of U.S. withdrawal of military support.

Haiti: Not only did the U.S. support two of the most brutal dictators Haiti has known ("Papa Doc" Duvalier and "Baby Doc" Duvalier), but numerous invasions of Haiti have been done for U.S. economic interests, which includes keeping the people enslaved and in abject poverty. The latest invasion with this purpose in mind was to overthrow the democratically-elected priest, Jean-Bertrand Aristide, in 2004. Meanwhile, Emmanuel Constant, a planner and organizer of terrorist brutality for the U.S. and against the citizens of Haiti, lives comfortably in New York, while the U.S. has either ignored or rejected all appeals from Haiti to return him for trial.[69]

Columbia: leading Western recipient of U.S. military aid, the government there has the worst human rights record in history, using chemicals on its own people, with the support of President Clinton (an alleged reason for the Iraq invasion by the U.S.).

Cuba: The U.S. policy toward Cuba, ever since Fidel Castro expelled the U.S.-backed Batista regime, can only be described as "terrorism." From Eisenhower on, the open policy of the United States has been to attempt to asphyxiate Cuba by strangling its citizens. Eisenhower directly stated that the Cuban people were responsible for the ongoing leadership of Castro, and that legitimated attacks on the civilians of Cuba in order to get Castro out of power.[70] In addition to that, there have been numerous embargoes, blockades, bombings, and other measures undertaken by the U.S., directly against the citizens of Cuba, that can only be described as terrorism: "attacks on fishing boats, embassies, Cuban offices overseas, the bombing of a Cuban airliners, killing all seventy-three passengers...and subsequent terrorist operations."[71]

Palestine and Gaza: U.S.-supported and approved attacks by Israel on these two enclaves, and U.S. support of the continuing building of Israeli settlements in the former, along with the late 2007 siege of, then fierce attack on the people Gaza goes so far beyond ambiguity as terrorist acts that one hesitates to add further detail in what is intended to be a sample list of U.S. terrorism. Just to keep with the most recent example, over 5,000 civilian deaths in a 25-mile strip of land, due to over 2,300 missile and bombing attacks by a U.S.-supplied Israeli military, in this, the most densely populated land on earth, is terrorism in upper-case letters. In addition, U.S.-Israel policy of eternal war on the Palestinians and Gaza, along with Lebanon, by refusal to accept a settlement returning to pre-June1967 borders, along with their rejection of the two state solution, U.S. vetoes on U.N. resolutions concerning Israeli actions, continual U.S. blocks of diplomatic resolutions (e.g. 1976 Syrian proposal; 2001 Taba negotiations; 2002 Saudi Plan; 2002 Geneva Accord); U.S. vetoes of Geneva Convention Contracting Parties calls to review what is going on in the occupied territories and to apply the Fourth Geneva Convention to these territories; and ignoring over 100 U.N. resolutions concerning Israeli actions against the Palestinians, along with U.S. support for Israel's blockades and sieges, are all direct attacks on civilians: terrorism by any other accounting.

Lebanon: U.S.-supported and approved attacks by Israel on Lebanon are well-documented and legion, especially in 1978, 1982, and most of all in 1985, the peak year for U.S.-approved attacks by Israel under the Reagan regime. Again, Israel attacked Lebanon in major raids in 1993, 1996, 2002, and 2007, directly attacking civilians.

Embracing murderers, terrorists, and thugs as rulers: The U.S. support of world leaders who routinely kill, torture, and abuse their people while doing what the U.S. orders them to do is extensive. A partial list would include Ferdinand Marcos of the Philippines, "Baby Doc" Duvalier of Haiti, Nicolae Ceausescu of Romania, Suharto of Indonesia, Mobutu Sese Seko of Zaire, Manuel Noriega, South Korean rulers, Saddam Hussein of Iraq, Vladimir Putin of Russia, etc.

Arms exports: The U.S. is by far the biggest exporter of weapons of destruction to other countries. A well-documented study from "Fast Facts" has drawn the following conclusions:[72]

> Since 1992, the United States has exported more than $142 billion dollars worth of weaponry to states around the world. [73] The U.S. dominates this international arms market, supplying just under half of all arms exports in 2001, roughly two and a half times more than the second and third largest suppliers.[74] U.S. weapons sales help outfit non-democratic regimes, soldiers who commit gross human rights abuses against their citizens and citizens of other countries, and forces in unstable regions on the verge of, in the middle of, or recovering from conflict.

Continuing on, the study finds that

> U.S.-origin weapons find their way into conflicts the world over. The United States supplied arms or military technology to more than 92% of the conflicts under way in 1999.[75] The costs to the families and communities afflicted by this violence is immeasurable. But to most arms dealers, the profit accumulated outweighs the lives lost. In the period from 1998-2001, over 68% of world arms deliveries were sold or given to developing nations, where lingering conflicts or societal violence can scare away potential investors.[76]

This listing is by no means exhaustive, nor as detailed as it might be. It serves merely to illustrate that by the definition of terrorism we have suggested, or even that allegedly embraced by the U.S., our country is the biggest terrorist in world society today.

Conclusion

The point of this book has been not that we *now* know the Bush administration lied to us and to the world in order to take the United States into an unnecessary war—i.e. a war of aggression upon the sovereign state of Iraq. Rather, the point has been that all of the issues and problems of their deceit were there from the start, and could have and should have been noticed, and in some cases, unmasked, by a thinking and ethically conscious public and media. That it was not is to our collective shame. That we can avoid this in the future is the point of this book. We cannot expect a significant change in this type of U.S. action in the world in the administration of President Barack Obama. Not only does the United States have a long history of unethical and illegal behavior toward other nations (some of which has been spelled out in this study), but Obama himself has pledged repeatedly to continue the "war on terrorism" (even in his inaugural speech), to step up the war in Afghanistan by deploying even more troops there, and has made no pledge to withdraw all troops from Iraq. So although Obama may nuance U.S. actions abroad, by no means does he plan to change them. It is up to us, the citizens of the U.S., to put pressure not just on Obama, but on our alleged Representatives and Congress people, to make the change needed. They will not do so by themselves. By understanding the complexity of the term "terrorism," and by engaging the tools of critical analysis and moral principle, we will be able to recognize our government's moral failures and their own terrorism, and then be in a position not to be led by the propaganda that the government and media use to direct our support for future wars. If we think these issues through by demanding more information and by weighing that information against the proposed action, and filtering it through the lens of ethical principles and international laws, we can stop our government from taking us down the dark road of wars of aggression and torture. It is our government, not theirs, and it is up to us to hold them accountable for their actions. With such information, critical thinking, and ethical consciousness, we can guide the U.S. back to a more positive relationship with the world, and restore democracy at home.

Notes

1. ABC News interview, October 11, 2005.
2. See Joshua Holland, "Right-Wingers are Defensive About Talk Radio Dominance," www.alternet.org, June 29, 2007.
3. Robert Dreyfus, "Leaving Iraq: Apocalypse Not," Washington Monthly, February 19, 2007. Unless otherwise noted, the analysis of the neocon position that follows is from Dreyfus.
4. Michael Duffy, "How to Walk Away," *Time*, July 20, 2007.
5. Ibid.
6. Chaim Kaufmann, "A Security Dilemma," *Harvard International Review*, Winter, 2007.
7. Johnson, Chalmers. *Nemesis: The Last Days of the American Republic* (New York: Metropolitan Books, 2007). See particularly Chapter Seven: "The Crisis of the American Republic."
8. Steven R. Weisman, "Powell Calls His Speech a Lasting Blot on His Record," *New York Times*, September 9, 2005.
9. By the numbers, that amounts to over 100 lies per person!
10. See Charles Lewis and Mark Reading-Smith, "False Pretenses," http://projects.publicintegrity.org/WarCard/, January 23, 2008. This study was not part of the one that comprises this book, because it is a retrospective study.
11. One of President Bush's lies in his State of the Union address on January 28, 2003.
12. *Today*, NBC, April 3, 2003
13. CNN, April 14, 2003
14. For details on the media as megaphone for government interests in these and other military adventures, see Norman Solomon, War Made Easy (Hoboken, New Jersey: John Wiley & Sons, Inc., 2005)
15. "In Iraq Crisis, Networks are Megaphones for Official Views, FAIR study, 3/18/03.
16. Habermas, *Between Facts and Norms*, p. 104.
17. Ibid.
18. Ibid., p. 124
19. Ibid., p. 444.
20. McGwire, International Affairs, January, 2005, as quoted in Noam Chomsky, *Failed States*, pg. 70.
21. Ibid.
22. Michael MccGwire, *International Affairs*, January, 2005, quoted in Chomsky, Norm, *Failed States*, pg. 70.
23. This is documented in detail in Noam Chomsky, *Hegemony or Survival*, passim.
24. Department of Defense, *Patterns of Global Terrorism*. Washington: Dept. of State, 2001: vi
25. 28 C.F.R. Section 0.85, http://www.fbi.gov/publications/terror/terror2000_2001.htm
26. Congressional Research Service, "Terrorism and National Security: Issues and Trends," *The Library of Congress*, October 2, 2003.
27. The definition was proposed by academic terrorist expert Alex P. Schmid, in 1988: United Nations, http://www.unodc.org/unodc/terrorism_definitions.html.

28. Alison Jaggar, "What is Terrorism, Why is it Wrong, and Could it Ever be Morally Permissible?," *Journal of Social Philosophy*, Summer, 2005, pgs. 202—217.
29. Chomsky, *Hegemony or Survival,* op. cit., p. 189.
30. U.N. Resolution 42/159, December 7, 1987. Quoted in Chomsky, *Hegemony or Survival*, op. cit., p. 190.
31. *Just and Unjust Wars*, op. cit., p. 197. He continues to hold this definition after 9/11/01. See "Five Questions About Terrorism," *Dissent*, Winter, 2002.
32. *Just and Unjust Wars*, p. 198.
33. Ibid., pgs. 251—252.
34. Ibid., p. 204.
35. Ibid., p. 203.
36. Ibid., p. 144.
37. He examines such historical episodes as the British bombing of German cities in WWII (p. 197), the Vietcong (pgs. 201—202), and the IRA (p. 203).
38. Ibid., p. 204.
39. Ibid., p. 254.
40. Ibid., p. 256.
41. Ibid., p. 203.
42. Ibid., p. 259.
43. Ibid., p. 200.
44. Ibid., p. 200.
45. Walzer, *Just and Unjust Wars*, p. 202.
46. Ibid., p. 203.
47. Ibid.
48. Ibid., p. 203.
49. Ibid., p. 262.
50. Ibid., p. 262.
51. Shannon E. French, "Murderers, Not Warriors," in Terrorism and International Justice, ed. James P. Sterba (Oxford: Oxford University Press, 2003), Chapter One.
52. Walzer, *Just and Unjust Wars*, op. cit., pgs. 255—262.
53. French, op. cit., p. 37.
54. While no listing would be complete or perhaps even sufficient, here are a few of the more interesting and thought-provoking writers who tackle the question of defining terrorism: Jenny Teichman, "How to Define Terrorism," *Philosophy*, October, 1989; Virginia Held, "Terrorism, Rights, and Political Goals," in R.G. Frey & Christopher Morris, ed. *Violence, Terrorism, and Justice* (New York: Cambridge University Press, 1991); David Rodin, "Terrorism Without Intention," *Ethics*, July, 2004; Samuel Scheffler, "Is Terrorism Morally Distinctive?" *The Journal of Political Philosophy*, vol. 14, n. 1, 2006; C.A.J. Coady, "The Morality of Terrorism," *Philosophy*, January, 1985.
55. Both Rodin and Scheffler do the same in their respective articles. Ibid.
56. Virginia Held, "Legitimate Authority in Non-state Groups using Violence," *Journal of Social Philosophy*, Summer, 2006, pgs. 175—193.
57. Ibid., p. 65.
58. Held, "Terrorism and War," p. 72.
59. Walzer, *Dissent*, op. cit.
60. Jaggar, op. cit., p. 209.
61. Ibid., p. 207.
62. Ibid., p. 208.

63. See Boyle, op. cit., p. 167.
64. Many of the episodes listed here are expounded upon in Chomsky, *Hegemony or Surivival*, op. cit., *passim*. Also in Chomsy, *Failed States*, op. cit., *passim*.
65. For more, see School of the Americas watch, www.soaw.org
66. For more, see Chomsky, *Failed States*, pgs. 155—158, and *passim*; and *Hegemony or Survival*, pgs. 95—108, and *passim*.
67. Chomsky, *Failed States*, p. 146.
68. Chomsky, *Failed States*, p. 150; *Hegemony or Survival*, p. 81.
69. *Failed States*, pgs. 154—155.
70. Ibid., pgs. 112—113.
71. Chomsky, *Hegemony or Survival*, p. 85.
72. From Fast Facts, www.fas.org.
73. Data compiled from addition of Foreign Military Sales (FMS) deliveries and Direct Commercial Sales (DCS) deliveries, FY1990-FY2000. a. "Foreign Military Sales, Foreign Military Construction Sales and Military Assistance Facts as of September 26, 2001." DSCA. Available online:DSCA 2001 Facts Book.
74. "Conventional Arms Transfers to Developing Nations, 1994-2001." CRS Report for Congress by Richard F. Grimmet. August 6, 2002. Order Code RL31529. Available online: Conventional Arms Transfers to Developing Nations.
75. World Policy Institute. Available online: www.worldpolicy.org You may also refer to "The New Business of War: Small Arms and the Proliferation of Conflict" by William D. Hartung. Published in Ethics & International Affairs, Vol. 15, No. 1, 2001. Online at www.cceia.org.
76. "Conventional Arms Transfers to Developing Nations, 1994-2001." CRS Report for Congress by Richard F. Grimmet. August 6, 2002. Order Code RL31529. Available online: Conventional Arms Transfers to Developing Nations.

Bibliography

Aljazeera. "Iraq War a 'Jihadist Cause Celebre," September 27, 2006.
American Academy of Arts & Sciences Committee on International Security Studies, "War with Iraq: Costs, Consequences, and Alternatives".
American Civil Liberties Union. "U.S. Operatives Killed Detainees During Interrogations in Afghanistan and Iraq,", October 24, 2005.
Archives of General Psychiatry, 2007 (from *Los Angeles Times*, "Psychological Torture Just as Bad, Study Finds," March 6).
Aristotle, *Politics* (trans. Richard McKeon) (New York: Random House, 1941).
Arkin, William M. "The Pentagon's Secret Scream," *The Los Angeles Times*, March 8, 2004.
Aquinas, Thomas. *Summa Contra Gentiles*, III (trans. James F. Anderson) (London: University of Notre Dame Press, 1956).
Asch, Solomon. "Opinions and Social Pressure," *Scientific American*, November, 1955.
Augustine, *City of God* (trans. Etienne Gilson) (New York: Image Books, 1958).
Bagaric, Mirko. "A Case for Torture," www.theage.com. The web version is an abbreviated form of a longer paper to be published by the University of San Francisco Law Review.
Bennis, Phyllis. "Powell's U.N. Presentation," *The Nation*, February 17, 2003.
Bentham, Jeremy. *An Introduction to the Principles of Morals and Legislation*. J.H. Burns and H.L.A. Hart, eds. (Oxford, Clarendon Press, 1970).
Blix, Hans. "Notes for Briefing the Security Council," http://www.un.org/Depts/unmovic.
Bookman, Jay, "The President's Real Goal in Iraq," *Information Clearinghouse*, September 29, 2002.
Bor, Jonathan. "654,000 Deaths Tied to Iraq War," *Baltimore Sun*, October 11, 2006.
Bramwell, Austin. "Good-bye to All That," *The American Conservative*, November 20, 2006.
Bush, George. *State of the Union Address,* January 28, 2003.
Bybee, Jay S. Memorandum for Alberto R. Gonzales, August 1, 2002. www.news.findlaw.com/nytimes/docs/doj/**bybee**80102mem.pdf
Carter, Jimmy. "Just War—or a Just War?" *New York Times*, March 9, 2003.
Chomsky, Noam. *Failed States* (New York: Metropolitan Books, 2006).

—. *Hegemony or Survival* (New York: Metropolitan Books, 2003).
Coady, C.A.J. "The Morality of Terrorism," *Philosophy*, January, 1985.
Coates, C.A.J. *The Ethics of War* (New York: Manchester University Press, 1997).
Cohn, Marjorie. "Redefining Torture," *Truthout*, January 3, 2005.
—. "Aggressive War: Supreme International Crime," www.truthout.org, November 9, 2004.
Cockburn, Alexander and Jeffrey St. Clair. "How Bush was Offered bin Laden and Blew it," *Counterpunch*, November 1, 2004.
Cockburn, Andrew. "How Rumsfeld Micromanaged Torture," *Counterpunch*, March 1-5, 2007.
Cockburn, Patrick. "U.S. Victory against Cult Leader was 'Massacre'," *The Independent/U.K.*, January 31, 2007.
Congressional Research Service, "Terrorism and National Security: Issues and Trends," *The Library of Congress*, October 2, 2003.
Cortright, David, Alistair Millar, George A. Lopez, and Linda Gerber, "Contested Case: Do the Facts Justify the Case for War in Iraq?" *A Report of the Sanctions and Security Project of the Fourth Freedom Forum and the Joan B. Kroc Institute for International Peace Studies at the University of Notre Dame*, February 6, 2003.
Currie, Duncan E.J. "Preventive War and International Law after Iraq," www.globelaw.com, May 22, 2003.
Cutler, Hugh Mercer. *Ethical Argument* (New York: Oxford University Press, 2004).
Danner, Mark. "The Logic of Torture," *The New York Review of Books*, June 24, 2004.
DeBelder, Bert. "Four Years into the Occupation: No Health for Iraq," *Global Policy Forum*, March 21, 2007;
Democracy Now! "Massacre in Haditha: Eight Marines Charged with Killing 24 Iraqis," December 22, 2006.
Democracy Now! "Star Wars in Iraq: Is the U.S. Using New Experimental Tactical High Energy Laser Weapons in Iraq?," July 25, 2006.
Democracy Now! "U.S. Broadcast Exclusive: "Fallujah: The Hidden Massacre' on the U.S. Use of Napalm-like White Phosphorus Bombs," November 8, 2005.
Department of Defense, *Patterns of Global Terrorism*. Washington: Dept. of State, 2001.
Donagan, Alan. *The Theory of Morality* (Chicago: The University of Chicago Press, 1977).
Dreyfus, Robert. "Leaving Iraq: Apocalypse Not," Washington Monthly, February 19, 2007.
—. "The Thirty-year Itch," *Mother Jones*, March/April, 2001.
Duffy, Michael. "How to Walk Away," *Time*, July 20, 2007.
Dworkin, Ronald. *Law's Empire* (Oxford: Hart Publishing, 1998).
—. *Taking Rights Seriously* (Cambridge: Harvard University Press, 1977).

El Baradei, Mohammed. "Status of the Agency's Verification Activities in Iraq as of 8 January 2003," http://www.iaea.org/worldatom/Press/Statements/2003

FAIR study, "In Iraq Crisis, Networks are Megaphones for Official Views," 3/18/03.

Foot, Philippa. "The Problem of Abortion and the Doctrine of Double Effect," *Virtues and Vices* (Berkeley and Los Angeles: University of California Press, 1978).

Foreign Military Sales (FMS) deliveries and Direct Commercial Sales (DCS) deliveries, FY1990-FY2000. a. "Foreign Military Sales, Foreign Military Construction Sales and Military Assistance Facts as of September 26, 2001."

French, Shannon E. "Murderers, Not Warriors," in *Terrorism and International Justice*, ed. James P. Sterba (Oxford: Oxford University Press, 2003).

Fuller, Lon. "The Forms and Limits of Adjudication," *Harvard Law Review*, 92 (1978).

Galston, William A. "The Perils of Preemptive War," *Philosophy & Public Policy Quarterly*, Vol. 22, n. 4, Fall, 2002.

Glantz, Aaron and Alaa Hassan. "U.S. Miltary Hides Many More Hadithas," *Inter-Press Service*, June 7, 2006.

Global Policy Forum. "Armed Groups Occupy Hospitals and Kidnap Doctors," February 13, 2007.

Goldenberg, Suzanne, Tania Branigan and Vikram Dodd, "Guantanamo Abuse Same as Abu Ghraib, say Britons," *The Guardian U.K.*, May 14, 2004.

Gonzalez, Alberto. "Decision Re Application of the Geneva Convention on Prisoners of War to the Conflict with Al Qaeda and the Taliban," January 25, 2002.

Grimmet, Richard F. "Conventional Arms Transfers to Developing Nations, 1994-2001." CRS Report for Congress August 6, 2002. Order Code RL31529.

Habermas, Jurgen. *Between Facts and Norms* (Cambridge, Mass: MIT Press, 1996).

—. *Knowledge and Human Interest* (Boston: Beacon Press, 1971).

—. "On the Employments of Practical Reason," *Justification and Application* (Cambridge, Mass: MIT Press, 2001).

Harding, Luke. "U.S. Military 'Brutalized' Journalists," *The Guardian U.K.*, January 13, 2004.

Hartung, William D "The New Business of War: Small Arms and the Proliferation of Conflict," Published in Ethics & International Affairs, Vol. 15, No. 1, 2001.

Hass, Ed. "FBI Says 'No Hard Evidence Connecting bin Laden to 9/11," *Muckracker Report*, June 6, 2006.

Hedges, Chris & Laila Al-Arian. "The Other War: Iraq Vets Bear Witness," *The Nation*, July 30, 2007.

Held, Virginia "Legitimate Authority in Non-state Groups using Violence," *Journal of Social Philosophy*, Summer, 2006.

—. "Terrorism, Rights, and Political Goals," in R.G. Frey & Christopher Morris, ed. *Violence, Terrorism, and Justice* (New York: Cambridge University Press, 1991)

Hendren, John. "Pentagon Files Reveal More Allegations of Abuse in Iraq," *The Los Angeles Times*, January 25, 2005.

Hersh, Seymour. "Torture at Abu Ghraib," *The New Yorker*, May 10, 2004.

Hirsh, Michael and John Barry. "The Salvador Option," *Newsweek*, January 8, 2005.

Hitchens, Christopher. "A War to be Proud Of," *The Weekly Standard*, September 5, 2005.

Hobbes Thomas. *Leviathan* (New York: Collier Books, 1962).

Holland, Joshua. "Right-Wingers are Defensive About Talk Radio Dominance," www.alternet.org, June 29, 2007.

Human Rights Watch Report, *The Road to Abu Ghraib*, June, 2004.

Jaggar, Alison. "What is Terrorism, Why is it Wrong, and Could it Ever be Morally Permissible?" *Journal of Social Philosophy*, Summer, 2005.

Jamal, Dahr. "Countless My Lai Massacres in Iraq," www.truthout.org, May 30, 2006.

Jamal, Dahr and Ali al-Fadhily. "Official Lies Over Najaf Battle Exposed," *Inter-Press Service*, February 1, 2007.

Johnson, Chalmers. *Nemesis: The Last Days of the American Republic* (New York: Metropolitan Books, 2007).

—. *Blowback* (New York: Metropolitan Books, 2000).

Kant, Immanuel. *Groundwork of the Metaphysic of Morals*, (trans. H.J. Paton) (New York: Harper Torchbooks, 1953).

Kaufmann, Chaim. "A Security Dilemma," *Harvard International Review*, Winter, 2007.

Klein, Naomi. "You Asked for my Evidence, Mr. Ambassador. Here it is," *The Guardian U.K.*, December 4, 2004

Kristof, Nicholas D. "Hitler on the Nile," *New York Times*, February 23, 2003.

Kruglanski A.W. & S. Fishman, "The Psychology of Terrorism: Syndrome versus tool perspective," *Journal of Terrorism and political Violence*, 2006.

Langan, John, S.J. "Is There a Cause for War Against Iraq?" November 13, 2002 (unpublished).

—. "Is There a Just Cause for War Against Iraq?" *State of the Nation*, Issue 4.1, Winter/Spring, 2003.

Lean, Geoffrey and Severin Carrell. "U.S. Prepares to Use Toxic Gases in Iraq," *The U.K. Independent*," March 2, 2003.

Lewis, Charles and Mark Reading-Smith. "False Pretenses," http://projects.publicintegrity.org/WarCard/, January 23, 2008.

Lewis, Neil A. "ACLU Presents Accusations of Serious Abuse of Iraqi Civilians," *The New York Times*, January 25, 2005.

Locke, John. *Two Treatises of Government* (ed. Peter Laslett) (New York: Cambridge University Press, 1988).

—. *Essays on the Law of Nature : The Latin Text with a Translation, Introduction and Notes, Together with Transcripts of Locke's Shorthand in his Journal for 1676*, W. von Leyden, ed, (Oxford University Press, 2002).

Mackay, Neil. "Why the CIA Thinks Bush is Wrong," *The Sunday Herald* (Scotland), October 13, 2002.

McCarthy, Rory and Julian Borger. "Taliban Ready to Strike a Deal on bin Laden," *Guardian*, February 22, 2001.

McCarthy, Rory. "U.S. Denies Need for Fallujah Aid Convoy," *The Guardian U.K.*, November 15, 2004.

McCoy. Alfred W. *A Question of Torture: CIA Interrogation, from the Cold War to the War on Terror*, 2006, Henry Holt and Company, New York.

—. "The Hidden History of CIA Torture," www.tomdispatch.com, September 10, 2004.

McGirk, Tim. "Collateral Damage or Civilian Massacre in Haditha?" *Time*, March 19, 2006.

McIntyre, Alison. "Doing Away with Double Effect," *Ethics*, January, 2001.

McKinnon, Barbara. *Ethics* (Belmont, California: Wadsworth, 2004).

Melzer, Yehuda. *Concepts of Just War* (Leyden: A.W. Sitjthoff, 1975).

Milgram, Stanley. *Obedience to Authority* (New York: Harper and Row), 1974.

Miraki, Mohammed Daud. "Perpetual Death from America," www.rense.com, February 24, 2003.

Moret, Leuren. "Depleted Uranium: Dirty Bombs, Dirty Missiles, Dirty Bullets," *San Francisco Bay View*, August 22, 2004.

Morgenthau, Hans. *Politics Among Nations* (New York: Alfred Knopf, 1954).

Myers, David G. *Social Psychology* (Boston: McGraw-Hill, 2005).

Nichols, John. "Dubious Dossier," *The Nation*, February 7, 2003.

Nichols, Thomas M. "Just War, Not Prevention," *Ethics & International Affairs*, 17.1 (April, 2003).

Nietzsche, Friedrich, *Twilight of the Idols,* from Walter Kaufmann, trans. *The Portable Nietzsche* (Penguin Books, 1982).

—. *Genealogy of Morals*, trans. Walter Kaufmann (New York: Vintage Books, 1969).

O'Connell, Mary Ellen. "The Myth of Preemptive Self-Defense," *The American Society of International Law*, August, 2002.

O'Hanlon, Michael E., Susan E. Rice, and James B. Steinberg. "The New National Security Strategy and Preemption," www.brookings.edu/comm/policybriefs/pb113.pdf, January, 2003.

Pape, Robert. "Dying to Kill Us," *New York Times*, September 22, 2003.

Parry, Robert. "Bush's Nuclear Gamble," Consortium News, September 30, 2002. Pincus, Walter. "CIA Learned in '02 That Bin Laden Had No Iraq Ties, Report Says," *Washington Post*, September 15, 2005.

Pojman, Louis. *Ethics: Discovering Right and Wrong*, (Belmont, California: Wadsworth, 1990).

Preston, Julia. "Inspector Says Iraq Falls Short," *New York Times*, January 28, 2003.

Price, Niko. "Iraq to Stop Counting Civilian Dead," *Associated Press*, December 10, 2003.
Rawls, John. *A Theory of Justice* (Cambridge: Harvard University Press, 1971).
—. *Law of Peoples* (Harvard University Press, 1999).
Risen, James. "Iraq Said to Have Tried to Reach Last-minute Deal to Avert War," *The New York Times*, November 6, 2003.
Rodin, David. "Terrorism Without Intention," *Ethics*, July, 2004
Scheffler, Samuel. "Is Terrorism Morally Distinctive?" *The Journal of Political Philosophy*, vol. 14, n. 1, 2006
Schwartz, Michael. "Is the United States Killing 10,000 Iraqis Every Month? Or is it More?" www.alternet.org, July 6, 2007.
Slaughter, Anne-Marie. "Good Reasons for Going around the U.N." *New York Times*, March, 18, 2003.
Smith, Dan. "Beyond Nuremberg: Crimes Against Peace," *Counterpunch*, August 11, 2006.
Solomon, Norman. *War Made Easy* (Hoboken, New Jersey: John Wiley & Sons, Inc., 2005).
Strauss, Leo. *What is Political Philosophy?* (Chicago: University of Chicago Press, 1959).
Sullivan, Andrew. "Soyster Speaks," The Atlantic, December 11, 2007.
Teichman, Jenny. "How to Define Terrorism," *Philosophy*, October, 1989
"The National Security Strategy of the United States of America," 2002, http://www.whitehouse.gov/nsc.
Thomas, Helen. "Attack on Fallujah can't be Justified," *Hearst Newspapers*, November 12, 2004.
Thucydides, *History of the Peloponnesian Wars: Revised Edition*. M. I. Finley, ed., Rex Warner, trans. (Penguin Classics, 1954).
Today, NBC, April 3, 2003.
U.N. News Centre, "Blix Welcomes Accelerated Cooperation by Iraq, but Says Unresolved Issues Remain," www.un.org, March 7, 2003.
U.N. Resolution 42/159, December 7, 1987.
U.S. Senate Resolution 3930, "The Military Commissions Act of 2006".
Wall Street Journal, July 25, 1985.
Walzer, Michael. "Five Questions About Terrorism," *Dissent*, Winter, 2002.
—. *Just and Unjust Wars* (Basic Books, 1977).
—. "What a Little War in Iraq Could Do," *New York Times*, March 7, 2003.
Weisman, Steven R. "Powell Calls His Speech a Lasting Blot on His Record," *New York Times*, September 9, 2005.
Whitaker, Brian. "American Troops are Killing and Abusing Afghans, Rights Body Says," *The Guardian*, March 8, 2004.
Wiener, Jon. "America's Complicity in Saddam's Crimes," *The Nation*, December 30, 2006.
Yerushalmi, David. "On Torture," *Intellectual Conservative*, October 4, 2006.

Index

Afghanistan, 1, 2, 20, 46, 51, 58, 59, 60, 63, 79, 83, 84, 85, 86, 101, 105
Al Qaeda, 8, 19, 20, 21, 22, 29, 31, 33, 46, 58, 63, 64, 79, 92, 96
bin Laden, 19, 20, 22, 64, 79
Blix, Hans, 17, 21, 24, 26, 27, 33, 34
Bush, George, 2, 15, 16, 21-24, 27, 29, 30-47 *passim*, 54, 55, 58, 59, 60, 68, 80, 82, 91, 96, 98-101 *passim*
Carter, Jimmy, 1, 30, 49
Chomsky, Noam, 38, 49, 100, 103, 116, 117, 118
civilians, viii, 31, 33, 51-58, 61, 63, 82, 83, 86, 87, 96, 101, 102, 104-113
Cohn, Marjorie, 55, 73, 74
consequences, 23, 35, 37, 39, 45-48, 51-53, 58-59, 81, 92, 93, 95, 97
Donagan, Alan, 48, 50
double effect, 51-53
El Baradei, Mohamed, 16, 21, 24, 33, 49
ethics/ethical, v-viii, 7, 23, 31, 39, 44, 45, 51, 53, 56, 61, 64, 66, 67, 77, 86, 94-97 *passim*, 100, 101, 114

evidence, v, vi, vii, 2, 15, 16-24, 26, 29-35, 59, 69, 70, 79, 80, 94-96, 98, 103, 111
fallacy, 34, 67, 68, 69, 95
Falluja, 55-57, 83, 104
Haditha, 55-57
Hitchens, Christopher, 31-33, 34-39, 49, 95
Hussein, Saddam, 1, 2, 9, 17-20, 21-24, 29, 31-43 *passim*, 57
IAEA, 19-21, 24-26, 33, 49, 95
imminent threat, vi, vii, 22, 24, 25, 34, 35, 36, 38-44 *passim*, 78-79
intention, vii, 40-41, 42, 45, 48, 51-54, 60, 61, 62, 88, 107
international law, viii, 22-25, 30, 31, 35-39, 42, 44, 56-62, 67, 77-89, 94-100, 105, 106, 111, 114
Iraqi civilian casualties, 55-57, 86, 87, 96
Israel, 21, 23, 37, 38, 46, 80, 85, 101, 103, 112-113
just cause, vi, viii, 10, 31-32, 34-36, 38, 41, 77, 78-80, 107, 110, 111
Just War, v-viii, 30-32, 34-36, 40-44, 77-79, 95, 97, 100-103, 106, 107
Langan, John, 31, 45, 49, 50

Index

legal, vi, 4, 10, 15, 19, 24-25, 31-37, 38, 42, 43, 59-61, 63, 66, 69, 71, 77, 78, 80, 83, 88, 94-99 *passim*
Locke, John, 6, 7, 8, 12, 100
logic/logical, 20, 24, 33, 34, 35, 36, 37, 41, 52, 65, 67, 70, 105
massacre, 38, 55, 56, 104
McCoy, Alfred W., 63, 68, 74
media, i, 26, 27, 79, 92, 94, 97-98, 119, 114
moral, vi-viii, 2-6, 12, 21-22, 30-31, 33-41, 44, 46, 48, 51-54, 58, 59, 61-71 *passim*, 77, 80, 83, 88, 93, 95, 97, 98, 101, 103-109 *passim*, 111, 114
neocons, 2, 3, 6-8, 91, 92
New York Times, 16, 22, 23, 24, 27, 28, 29, 30, 49, 50, 73, 74, 97, 116
Nichols, Thomas, 31-38, 44, 45, 49, 50
noncombatants, vii, 30, 55, 51-58, 107-110
Pape, Robert, 65, 74
Powell, Colin, 16-21, 22, 24, 28, 42, 94, 96, 116
preventive vs. preemptive wars, 9, 33-35, 39-40, 41-46, 58, 80, 95
principles (moral), vi, vii, 2, 6, 9, 30, 31, 35-38, 40, 41, 44, 51, 52, 53, 56, 59, 61, 66, 68, 71, 77, 79, 88, 94, 95, 97, 98, 100, 101, 105, 106, 107, 114
proportionality, vi, vii, viii, 30, 48, 52, 53, 54, 58-59, 86, 106
Rice, Condoleeza, 2, 16, 42, 96
rights, 8, 31, 40, 60-61, 63, 69, 70-71, 80, 83, 84, 86, 99, 102, 107, 112, 113

Strauss, Leo, 2-8, 10, 12
sufficient condition, 36, 48, 93, 101, 107, 108
terrorism/terrorist, 8, 10, 15, 19, 22, 23, 24, 29, 30, 32, 33, 34, 37, 40, 41, 46, 54, 56, 58, 60, 67
torture, 23, 57, 58, 59-72, 81, 83, 87, 88, 94, 96, 113, 114
United Nations/U.N., 9, 15-17, 19, 21, 23-31, 33, 35-38, 41-45, 49, 61-63, 77-80, 94-95, 100-103, 111, 113, 116
UNMOVIC, 15, 18, 19, 21, 25, 26, 27, 33, 49
U.N. Resolutions, 15, 16, 17, 19, 21, 25, 26, 31, 33, 43, 44, 80-81, 95, 100, 103, 105, 111, 113
U.S. Constitution, 43-44
values, 7, 35-36, 38, 39, 54, 66, 71, 97, 104
Walzer, Michael, 29, 38-40, 42, 44, 49, 50, 53-54, 56, 64, 73, 74, 77, 89, 98, 103-110, 116
weapons of mass destruction (WMD), i, viii, 2, 9, 15-21, 31-34, 37, 41, 42, 46, 47, 59, 94, 96, 97
chemical weapons, 15, 17, 18, 22, 23-27, 33, 34, 57, 59, 64, 112
biological weapons, viii, 10, 15, 16, 18, 21, 22, 25, 26, 33, 34
nuclear weapons, viii, 9, 15, 19, 20-26 *passim*, 29, 32, 33, 34, 37, 38, 40, 44, 47, 64, 80, 99, 100
Zarqawi, 19, 22, 29, 32, 39, 95

About the Author

Dr. Robert Abele holds a Ph.D. in Philosophy from Marquette University and M.A. degrees in Theology and Divinity. He is the recipient of numerous scholarships and fellowships, including the National Endowment for the Humanities Fellowship to the U.S. Naval Academy for the study of war and morality (2004), and the Illinois Council of Humanities Scholarship in, for his work on the issues of freedom and democracy (2003). He is the author of three books: *A User's Guide to the USA PATRIOT Act* (2005); *The Anatomy of a Deception: A Logical and Ethical Analysis of the Decision to Invade Iraq* (2009); and *Democracy Gone: A Chronicle of the Last Chapters of the Great American Democratic Experiment* (2009), and numerous articles on politics and U.S. government foreign and domestic policies. Dr. Abele is an instructor of philosophy at Diablo Valley College, located in Pleasant Hill, California in the San Francisco Bay area.